Be Still

Stress & Anxiety Management for Latter-day Saints

Dr. Victoria Anderson

Lois D. Brown

Levanter Publishing

www.levanterpublishing.com

ISNB: 978-0-9847237-6-8

AUTHORS' NOTE:

The names of all individuals mentioned in this book were changed or left out intentionally. This book was written to give accurate and helpful information in regard to the subject matter. It is not intended to diagnose or to treat physical or mental health problems of any kind. The authors encourage readers to seek professional medical healthcare and to employ the services of a competent mental health professional.

DEDICATION

To Joseph and McKay

TABLE OF CONTENTS

INTRODUCTION

In the book *Way to Be*, former president of the LDS Church Gordon B. Hinckley observed, "We are entitled to spend some time with ourselves... Find some time to drown out the noise of the world."[1] Yet many Latter-day Saints are rarely still. We are too busy being fathers, mothers, husbands, wives, grandparents, bishops, nursery workers, compassionate service leaders, food storage experts, scripture scholars, and the list goes on. Historically, religion has been referred to as an "opiate to the masses." To Latter-day Saints, however, it seems more like an amphetamine.

Stress and anxiety are no "respecter of persons" (D&C 38:16). Together they affect 100 percent of the population, and stress is the number one reason people visit the doctor. Studies estimate that 75 to 90 percent of all visits to primary care physicians are for stress-related problems. Latter-day Saints are no different.

Chronic stress contributes to health problems such as heart disease (including strokes), Alzheimer's disease, and diabetes. A study by Harvard University reported that 50 percent of all Americans will suffer psychological symptoms that qualify for a diagnosis of mental illness at some time in their lives.[2] Stress is a major contributor to this fact.

At times, depending upon our physical, emotional, mental, and spiritual well-being, stress can turn into anxiety. Anxiety is the most common of all the mental health problems. One in every eight people in the United States currently has a moderate to serious problem with anxiety. Many others suffer from mild anxiety. Anxiety can result in recurrent panic attacks. Anxiety can also stem from chronic depression or turn into depression. Research shows that approximately 60 percent of people who suffer from depression also have anxiety.[3]

Everyone is susceptible to stress and anxiety because these conditions are connected to our genetic makeup. Yet some Latter-day Saints feel guilt and shame when they experience these conditions. Those who recognize their unease as anxiety related don't often talk about it because they believe it may appear as a character flaw or as a lack in faith. Many members feel they must hide their stress or anxiety. They believe by sharing their struggles they appear foolish and weak. Nothing is further from the truth.

Chronic stress and anxiety are common, treatable conditions. In this book are forty-four techniques to manage the physical, emotional, mental, and spiritual symptoms that accompany stress and anxiety. Most texts on stress and anxiety do not cover the spiritual aspect to these conditions. We believe, however, effective management of anxiety occurs when we address the condition from all areas in our life. If we leave one area untouched, we often miss out on a critical aspect to the healing process.

Research supports the power of combining spiritual healing with physical and emotional healing. Scientists studied two groups of Christian clients with depression and anxiety. The first group was given standard therapy. The second group was given religiously oriented therapy. The largest reduction in depression and anxiety was from the group of Christians given the religiously oriented therapy.[4] Strengthening ourselves spiritually is essential when seeking physical, emotional, *and* mental healing.

We are told in the *Doctrine and Covenants* to "...be anxiously engaged in a good cause" (D&C 58:27), and we are told in the *Book of Mormon* that "it is not requisite that a man should run faster than he has strength" (Mosiah 4:27). This book will help you find the balance between these two counsels. As Elder Jeff Holland, a member of the Quorum of the Twelve, has said, "To raise our families and serve faithfully in the Church, all without running faster than we have strength, requires wisdom, judgment, divine help, and inevitably some sacrifice."[5] *Be Still* is designed to help Latter-day Saints gain the strength, wisdom, and judgment necessary to receive divine help in relation to their stress and anxiety challenges.

As we learn the art of stillness, we accomplish more, feel better about ourselves, and enjoy life more completely.

CHAPTER ONE— Stress: Primeval or Modern?

As Laura sat on the couch watching a video with her husband and children, she felt her stomach churn. She had so much to do the next few days and didn't know how she would get it all done. As she thought about upcoming commitments, her stomach tightened even more. "Try and relax," she told herself, but inside she kept thinking about her busy schedule.

Ron was supposed to be concentrating on driving, but instead his mind was racing about a problem at work. His hands felt clammy, and his heart beat faster. He felt tense, knowing he was headed for another late night on the computer distracted from his family and church calling. But if he didn't solve the problems at work, who would? When would he stop feeling like his life was out of control?

Dave was facing a confusing future. He had just been diagnosed with cancer. His thoughts often dwelt on the possibility of death and the inability to support his family. He didn't want to be a burden. He found himself asking, "Why me? Why is God punishing me? Why won't He cure me so I can live a healthy life?" He physically felt sick to his stomach, dizzy, and had major headaches. Verbally he attributed these symptoms to the cancer, but deep down he knew they were connected to his anxiety about the future.

Anne lay with her eyes open, but the room was dark. Two weeks ago her life had seemed normal—taking care of her toddler, teaching part-time at the local university, and spending a lot of time in her ward with the young women. Life was full. It hadn't mattered that she was six months pregnant and feeling under the weather. Then she had started having trouble sleeping, and it had gone from bad to worse. Now it had been several days since she had slept at all. Her body was exhausted, but whenever she tried to rest she jerked awake, feeling panicked. Was she going crazy? Was Heavenly Father punishing her for not doing everything right? Why did she feel so much anxiety and panic?

Laura, Ron, Dave and Anne assume their stress is caused by a weakness of character and the inability to handle life. What they don't realize is that while discussion about stress and anxiety has increased over the past thirty years, the conditions themselves have been around for thousands of years.

The *Old Testament* prophet Moses never used a computer and he never drove a car, but experienced similar feelings of stress as Laura, Ron, Dave and Anne.

In the *Pearl of Great Price*, we read about when Moses was transfigured so he could stand to be in the presence of God. He was told he had an important work to do on earth and then shown the magnitude of the world. Afterward, he "fell unto the earth. It was for the space of many hours before Moses did again receive his natural strength" (Moses 1:9-10). At a time when Moses was feeling physically exhausted and mentally and emotionally overwhelmed, who decided to show up? The adversary.

"Satan came tempting him, saying: Moses, son of man, worship me"

(Moses 1:12).

But Moses knew better, and he told Satan. "I can judge between Him and thee. Depart hence, Satan" (Moses 1:18).

Satan, however, didn't give up that easy. He began to cry with a loud voice and rant and rave. He demanded Moses worship him.

"And it came to pass that Moses began to fear exceedingly; and as he began to fear, he saw the bitterness of hell" (Moses 1:20).

How could Moses fear? He had just seen God the Father. He even voiced aloud that he could tell the difference between God's presence and Satan's. Did Satan have any real power over him? All Satan could do was rant and rave, yet Moses "began to fear exceedingly."

What was it that Moses feared? Possibly Moses began to doubt himself. Satan was only more than happy to encourage this self-doubt, reminding Moses that he was merely a "son of man" (Moses 1:12). Perhaps Moses began to wonder if he could accomplish all that was needed of him. Perhaps he began to question Heavenly Father's choice of calling him to the work.

Moses had all the ingredients for anxiety: 1) he was physically weakened 2) he was emotionally drained 3) he was mentally feeling out of control of the situation and 4) his spiritual self was being beaten down by Satan.

Moses found hope and help in his time of desperation. "Nevertheless, calling upon God, he received strength" (Moses 1:20). Eventually Moses became the beloved prophet of the Israelites. He gained the self-assurance to become an instrument in the hand of God. He comforted others when they were tried and tested, and he fulfilled the work that Father in Heaven gave him to do.

ANXIETY THROUGHOUT THE AGES

Throughout history, Moses was not alone. Famous medical scholar, Hippocrates, attempted to explain the conditions of fear, panic, and anxiety. In 400 B.C. he used words such as "melancholia" to describe patients suffering from stress and depression. He hypothesized that "from the brain... arise our pleasures, joys... as well as our sorrows, pains, grief, and tears. It is the same organ which makes us mad or delirious, inspires us with dread and fear, brings sleeplessness...and aimless anxiety."[6]

The dark ages were full of mystic spells believed to conjure calmness from unrest and anxiousness. The Renaissance brought about a more realistic, though very elementary understanding, of anxiety and stress. And in our not-so-distant past, there was Sigmund Freud. At the turn of the 19th Century, not only did Dr. Freud treat people for anxiety, but his personal writings indicate he most likely suffered from the condition himself.[7]

By looking at the origins of some words involved with stress, we see just how far back the condition existed in society. The word "anxiety" comes from the Latin word "angere" that means to choke. A common physical reaction of anxiety feels like choking. The word "panic" comes from the Greek god named Pan. According to Greek mythology, when a person woke Pan from his sleep, he caused the person overwhelming and intense fear. The word "agoraphobia" comes from ancient Greece. In Greek, "agora" means marketplace or a place where people gather and "phobia" means fear. Agoraphobia literally means a fear of the marketplace. In today's world, an agoraphobic is someone who, because of a fear of panicking in a public situation, chooses to stay confined to his or her home.

Walter Cannon, in 1914, was the first person to use the word "stress" in a medical context. Before that, the word had only been used by engineers to describe the mechanical force placed on a physical object. Just a few years later, Dr. Han Seyle popularized the word and introduced it to the American household. The word stress is now used by nearly everyone, every day. But knowing what a words means versus how it applies to us individually is not the same. We all feel stress a little differently.

The individuals you met in the first of this chapter—Laura, Dave, Ron, and Anne— are real, intelligent, and successful people. However, they all needed to learn how to better manage their stress and anxiety—the same task that has faced millions of people before them for thousands of years.

Thankfully, scientists now understand the brain and the body better than ever before. Certain physical, emotional, mental, and spiritual techniques have been researched, studied, and proven to help people manage their stress and anxiety. We will discuss forty-four of these techniques in the chapters of this book.

For example, Laura's desire to be liked by everyone fueled her inability to say "no." When we fear internally what others might think about us, we often do more than we are physically able. Some people, like Laura, have such an aversion to saying "no" that they become consumed with obligations and feelings of being overwhelmed.

Ron's chronic stress over problems at work was turning into anxiety. Ron learned that by changing various work habits and by employing various physical anxiety-reducing techniques, his drive home from work could be a lot less stressful, and he could enjoy his family more at home.

Dave's anxiety was connected to his thinking patterns and a frightening illness. His worries about his future were taking over his ability to think of anything else. His health, which was already compromised by the cancer, was also in jeopardy from the stress. As he learned to change his thought process and connect to his spiritual faith, his physical body could better fight the cancer. We better manage stress when we distinguish between what we can control and what we can't.

Anne's anxiety related insomnia was the result of factors that had been building in her life for decades. While the anxiety was triggered by hormone changes in pregnancy (anxiety is most common in women during pregnancy and up to two years after as well as in menopause), her continued panic was rooted in traumatic childhood experiences. Not only did Anne have to treat some of her physical symptoms of anxiety, but she also had to come to terms with her own emotional insecurity.

By recognizing and learning how to deal with physical, emotional, mental, and spiritual symptoms of stress and anxiety, we will have the ability to calm ourselves. Stillness is achieved by working through tangible, proven anxiety-reducing techniques and by giving back our control to a loving Heavenly Father.

CHAPTER TWO—The Nuts and Bolts

In the scriptures, stress and anxiety go by many different names: fear, dread, sorrow, suffering, troubled, calamity, tribulation, vexation, etc.

We read of individuals whose anxiety is brought on by sin, like the fear Sherem, the anti-Christ, felt at the end of his life when in Jacob 7: 19 he confesses, "...and because I have thus lied unto God I greatly fear." Other times, however, anxiety is not related to sin, as was the case with Moses (see Chapter One).

While individuals feel stress differently, the physiological reaction in the body is almost always the same. Simply put, stress is the effect of the body releasing heightened levels of adrenalin and cortisol, two hormones made by the adrenal gland. These hormones trigger the "flight or fight" response and prepare a person for a dangerous situation.

A natural increase in these hormones brings about the same response as injecting the body with a synthetic stimulant such as cocaine or similar powerful drugs. Someone taking drugs feels agitated, tense, and even frantic after the initial high. It's the same with someone experiencing chronic stress and anxiety.

Chronic stress, anxiety, and anxiety-related depression are

conditions more than half of Americans experience at moderate to severe levels sometime during their lifetime.

Depression and Anxiety

The National Institute of Mental Health estimates that anxiety affects about twenty million Americans and depression affects about nineteen million. The two are cousins, if not siblings. In about half of diagnosed cases, depression and anxiety are both present.

Just like the chicken and the egg, some ask, "Which comes first? The depression or the anxiety?" In reality, it doesn't matter. What helps one condition usually helps the other. Treating the two conditions together is just as common as treating them separately.

However, there are some shared symptoms to both conditions and some symptoms that are unique. Problems such as insomnia, restlessness, irritability, fatigue, and difficulty concentrating are symptoms associated with both depression and anxiety. Anxiety, however, has additional symptoms such as feelings of fear, panic, obsessive thinking, painful memories, and physical ailments. Depression is a disorder that affects a person's mood. With depression, lethargy and a disconnection from people are often present. People with anxiety are typically highly self-aware, even to the point of recognizing their irrational thoughts and behaviors. They often are extremely body sensitive and feel their physical symptoms intensely, while those who are depressed sometimes don't even realize they are in the throws of depression.

The Limbic System

The limbic system is found within the brain and is made up of several important cortical structures. Some of these structures include the hippocampus (required for the formation of long-term memories), the hypothalamus (a gland that regulates the autonomic nervous system through hormone production) and the amygdala (involved in aggression and fear).

The amygdala constantly scans surrounding stimuli for danger. The hippocampus may aid the amygdala in this task by associating a current situation to a fearful long-term memory. When the amygdala senses danger (whether real or perceived) first it immediately tells the hypothalamus to increase production and distribution of adrenaline and cortisol (the two stress hormones).

Second, the amygdala sends a message to the brain to shut down all blood flow to the prefrontal cortex of the brain (where our logic and creativity centers are located). By doing this, the amygdala single-handedly places the body into a position to either fight or flight—a panic reaction.

Left unattended, a panic reaction lasts a few minutes to possibly twenty minutes. However, an over-stimulated amygdala may continue to send panic messages to the brain as long as it perceives danger is present, thereby creating a panic cycle (otherwise known as chronic stress or anxiety).

Types of Anxiety

Anxiety is an umbrella term that technically describes various stages of limbic stimulation. Let's take a minute to review the types and levels of stress and anxiety:

Acute stress lasts a relatively short period of time and is brought on by specific circumstances. Acute stress can demand all of our energy and leaves us drained and fatigued. In some cases, acute stress can cause a state of shock. Examples of acute stress can be attributed to a deadline at work, an accident or unexpected trauma, or even an adverse reaction to medication.

Chronic stress extends for a longer period of time and is often present as we perform daily activities. Often, our bodies react to chronic stress slowly, and we might even become accustomed to a certain level of tension. This stress is harmful because it can lead to chronic illness such as ulcers or heart disease. Chronic stress is often ignored until the body shows symptoms such as an increase in headaches or fatigue. People who suffer from chronic stress might feel depressed or incapable of getting through the day. They may also suffer from high blood pressure, insomnia, or irritability.

One client came in complaining of anxiety and headaches. She had recently been going back to school to complete a degree as well as caring for three disabled children. She often stayed up late studying and was getting less than six hours of sleep at night. This routine created chronic stress with physical symptoms that increased over time. Lifestyle changes over time slowly eliminated her physical symptoms and her ability to better handle life. She started by getting more sleep and cutting back on the number of classes she took. She also came up with alternative ways to have more help in taking care of her disabled children. These changes helped to make a difference in her level of chronic stress and, consequentially, her overall physical health.

Anxiety is a response to stress that produces a state of fearfulness and distressing physical symptoms. Most people suffer from short periods of anxiety during moments prior to examinations or job interviews. This type of anxiety does not usually persist. When anxiety fails to go away, or if it is disproportionate to the severity of the situation, it can dramatically affect everyday life. Anxiety can be mild, moderate, or severe.

Dr. Edmund Bourne, author of *The Anxiety Workbook*, reports mild anxiety does not significantly interfere with the ability to work or maintain important relationships. Mild anxiety is disturbing, but it does not cause overwhelming and constant distress. Moderate to severe anxiety, on the other hand, disrupts a person's life enough that it's difficult to get to work or function well on the job. It may cause relationship difficulties, and it causes distress at least 50 percent of the time a person is awake.[8]

Panic is acute and extreme anxiety with accompanying physiologic symptoms. Panic can be a part of acute stress, chronic stress, and anxiety. One male client sought therapy because of his severe panic reaction to speaking in public. He became so anxious while talking to large groups that he felt he would pass out or have a heart attack. This fear continued to get worse until he took a leave of absence from his work. He received treatment and medication and learned to manage his panic reaction effectively. He was eventually able to go back to work and speak successfully to large groups without panicking.

The following anxiety scale may help people recognize the levels of stress and anxiety they experience.[9]

Stress and Anxiety Scale

Relaxed: Internal calm; undistracted; peaceful; clear thoughts.

Mild Stress: Rushed; slightly nervous; feeling somewhat overburdened.

Stress/mild anxiety: Butterflies in stomach; muscle tension; nervousness; feeling of being overwhelmed.

Moderate anxiety: Heartbeat quickens; rapid breathing begins; sweating; possible tingling in extremities; physical symptoms of anxiety are uncomfortable but person still feels somewhat in control.

Marked Anxiety: Feelings of discomfort heighten; mind and body disconnection begins; muscles either very tight or shaky; person begins to feel a large loss of control.

Panicky: Difficult to breath; dizzy; detached, disoriented; heart pounding and beating irregularly; strong feelings and fear and of losing total control.

Panic Attack: Heart palpitations; short breathes; choking sensation; major shaking in legs and arms; need to get out or get away; sense of control is completely gone; thoughts of dying; thoughts of going crazy; complete detachment from body; possible feelings of terror.

The effects of stress, anxiety, and panic can build up over time. All change produces stress, whether positive or negative. However, when we are physically, emotionally, mentally, and spiritually healthy we may not notice the small stressors (external events) in our lives, and we will be able to better manage the bigger stresses.

No matter what type of anxiety or stress a person may have, the techniques in this book will work as a multi-faceted stress management plan. If anxiety levels are moderate to severe, individuals may also benefit from involving a professional therapist. It doesn't matter who or where we are in life, stress and anxiety are two things we can all learn to manage more effectively for better physical, mental, and spiritual health.

Ironically, even saying the word "anxiety" may provoke fear in some people. Chelsea had her first serious bout of anxiety in high school. Since that time, she says she doesn't use the word anxiety because of the reaction she gets from others.

"People tell me when I say the word anxiety, it gives them anxiety," she says. "So I just try to avoid talking about it." Other people feel that admitting they are stressed is like divulging some sign of weakness or inability to cope.

Sometimes we forget that all anxiety is not bad. It is the reason most of us are able to make things happen. A small amount of anxiety rouses us to action. It gears us up to face uncomfortable situations. It helps us stay standing when giving a talk in sacrament meeting. It gives us the energy needed to compete in sports or the motivation to study for an exam.

Here is a surprising fact—stress isn't all bad either. In the right dosage, stress may actually increase health. A recent study done at Duke University showed that stress can "prime the immune the system" and make us stronger, more resilient to physical disease or additional stress.

Take for instance the person who, despite suffering from a chronic illness, manages to get up every day and do his job. In fact, when the job is taken away from him, his health also declines. The stress of the job actually gets the immune system working and allows the person to function. One researcher tried to validate this phenomenon in a laboratory experiment. He exposed rats to a certain type of contagious bacteria. Some of the rats were given an added dose of stress that came in the form of an electric shock. The rats given the electric shocks resisted the disease longer than rats that did not receive shocks.[10]

Even panic has its useful function. Most people panic when an extremely stressful situation arises. Let's say you're driving down the freeway when the car in front of you spins out of control. Without consciously thinking about it, your body starts a panic reaction that tells your foot to press on the brake and your arms to swerve the steering wheel. Panic can help us avoid danger. Panic in a non-threatening situation is described as a panic attack (also called an anxiety attack). A panic attack is an exaggeration of our body's emergency response system when there is no real danger present.

While it's true that some stress and anxiety is beneficial, chronic stress or anxiety isn't. This is where it gets complicated. Wouldn't it be great if we could buy a stress patch that turned a different color when our stress reaction reached a dangerous level? In reality, a "stress patch" couldn't work universally because we each have our own stress zone in which we function well. For some people, a normal stress zone may be another person's panic zone—everyone's reaction to stress is different because of their genetic makeup and environment.

Each of us needs to learn how to live within our normal stress zone. When internal or external factors happen that push us outside our normal zone, we may end up with symptoms of anxiety or chronic stress that disrupt daily activities and thoughts. These symptoms serve as red flags that we are functioning outside of our acceptable stress zone, and we need to slow things down.

Unfortunately, many of us ignore symptoms of stress or anxiety until they grow into a self-feeding cycle. A self-feeding cycle is when we get stressed about the fact that we are stressed or anxious. In this situation, we need tools to feel more in control of our body's responses to built-up stress.

A client, Jerry, came into treatment complaining of panic attacks and difficulty sleeping. Jerry was a successful business man who functioned very well, but over time his stress had built up until he was experiencing high levels of anxiety and panic feelings. Jerry was a Vietnam veteran who had worked in Special Operations during the war. He had learned to suppress feelings as a coping mechanism during his military service.

Jerry did not have any close friends and he was not close to his family. He reported having difficulty concentrating and being able to sleep through the night. He also frequently lost his temper. His symptoms had increased until his anxiety had become disabling. He felt completely out of control of his life.

Together, Jerry and I learned that his problems with anxiety were due to repressed emotions and a family history of anxiety. With medication and therapy, Jerry was able to feel normal again and deal with the stress of daily life. He returned to his normal stress zone where he functioned very well.

Many times the combination of heredity, a pre-disposition to anxiety, plus life stress that has been repressed or not dealt with completely can cause periods of anxiety, depression, or emotional shut down. Eventually our inner being has a way of making us face past traumas, work through them, learn from them, and eventually move on.

Jerry learned to connect with repressed feelings and to grieve losses in his life. This helped him draw closer to his own family and make new friends. Feelings were no longer threatening to him, and consequently his anxiety about expressing feelings decreased to a manageable level. His anxiety symptoms were really a wake-up call telling him it was time to change and grow.

Recognizing the Symptoms and Causes

Learning about stress and anxiety takes away the mystery and fear associated with them. Unfortunately, few people recognize what their stress or anxiety symptoms are until those symptoms are strong enough to disrupt their lives. Imagine if a car's oil light didn't work. Some of us would never bother to check the oil and we would drive the car until the motor was destroyed. It is the same with our bodies.

Since recognizing stress symptoms is crucial to our well-being, let's discuss the different ways stress and anxiety manifest themselves in our lives. Recognize that stress and anxiety symptoms are not the same for everyone.

Physiological Symptoms

Many people have physical symptoms that may be mild but then increase until they feel physically ill. For instance, one man went to his primary care physician complaining of constant numbness in his hands or feet. He was baffled when tests for nerve damage came back negative. Instead he was told he had anxiety. Another woman went to countless doctors and took dozens of tests to determine why she had severe dizziness. At last her internist suggested she may have postpartum depression, a condition in which anxiety can often play a role.

Rarely does someone experience all of the bodily or physiological symptoms listed. Instead, everyone tends to have a unique set of stress and anxiety symptoms. Some of these symptoms may be the result of health issues other than anxiety, so if you have persistent symptoms you should have a full medical exam to see if there are other health conditions present. These symptoms can become chronic, meaning we experience them even when we do not necessarily feel anxious.

Many of the physical symptoms of stress and anxiety are caused by the rapid movement of blood. In a stressful situation, the body will 1) move the blood quickly from the frontal lobes of the brain to the base of the brain, and 2) move blood from the extremities and stomach to critical organs such as the heart and lungs. This transfer of blood flow can cause unusual, disturbing, and frightening symptoms.

Physiological reactions to stress and anxiety may include:

- backaches
- churning in stomach
- difficulty sleeping
- dizziness
- dry mouth
- fatigue
- headaches
- high blood pressure
- jaw tension
- lightheadedness
- migraines
- muscle jerking
- muscle spasms
- rapid heartbeat
- sweating
- tense muscles
- tightness around eyes
- tingling in extremities
- upset stomach
- digestive problems

Physiological reactions that may happen during panic may include:

- blurred vision
- chilled body
- depersonalization (dream-like state)
- derealization (detached)

- difficulty swallowing
- extreme dizziness
- fainting
- heart palpitations
- hyperventilation
- nausea
- numbness in hands/arms
- pain in chest
- shaking legs/arms/hands
- dry mouth
- trembling voice
- vertigo

A young man came in for treatment for paralysis in his right arm. The paralysis came on suddenly after a life-threatening situation. Medical tests showed no logical reason for his disability. This extreme reaction to anxiety and stress is called a conversion reaction. "In a conversion reaction, the individual protects himself against some anxiety-arousing situation by developing the symptoms of a disease or disability. . . no organic pathology underlies such symptoms."[11]

With treatment and possible medications, in most cases the symptoms in a conversion reaction are eliminated. This is a very rare physical reaction to a stressful and traumatic situation.

<u>Behavioral Symptoms</u>

Behavioral reactions to stress or anxiety also vary greatly from person to person. There are two types of stress-related behavioral changes: A person stops former behaviors (an avoidance behavior) or begins new behaviors (a nervous behavior).

For example, Lynn enjoyed swimming until he saw something traumatic happen at a swimming pool. He then did whatever he could do to avoid swimming. This is an avoidance behavior. On the hand, Samantha enjoyed college until she took a math class that was difficult and stressful. When she started to do her math homework, she began to severely bite her fingernails. She developed this nervous behavior unconsciously to help the body relieve stress and anxiety.

Nervous behaviors from stress and anxiety may include:

- fiddling with objects
- irritability
- over eating/not eating
- talking too much
- fingernail biting
- picking at blemishes
- trichotillo
- fainting

Avoidance behaviors can happen when a person experiences severe anxiety at a specific time or in a certain place. Common places or behaviors people may avoid include but are not limited to:

- being alone
- crowded places
- intimate situations
- public social situations
- cars
- confined places
- people in general
- former place of trauma

One woman I helped had an extreme nervous reaction to stress and anxiety. She would actually lose consciousness. Her fainting coincided with a stressful social situation such as speaking in public or going to places where there were large crowds. Once she learned skills to deal with her anxiety, her fainting stopped.

Psychological Symptoms

When we have chronic stress and anxiety, our thinking may change as the condition persists. On the other hand, learned negative thinking may even be the root or cause of the anxiety itself. Whichever the case, anxious thoughts typically dwell on imperfections, weaknesses, and the uncertainty of the future. When anxious, we ask a lot of negative "what if" questions. "What if I mess up in my meeting today?" or "What if my children don't make it home from school safely?" Anxious thoughts usually escalate. An anxious person tends to magnify problems until they become the majority of what he or she thinks about.

Some common anxious negative thoughts usually begin with:

- I can't do that.
- I'm not as capable as he/she is.
- I'm not good enough.
- I'm so overwhelmed.
- What I think doesn't matter.
- What if…
- When will this just go away?
- Why can't I…

During an anxiety or panic attack, the mind usually focuses on the worst case scenario. The mind will focus its thoughts on three types of thoughts:

1. Past times of panic. This reminds us how awful the panic felt and makes us try to fight the panic so it won't come again.
2. The uncomfortable feelings the body is experiencing. Dwelling on this often makes the symptoms worse.
3. The future and the fear of what will happen if the panic never stops.

These types of thoughts compound the problem. During panic, we tend to ignore reasonable explanations.

Some common thoughts during a panic attack may be:

- I'm going to die.
- I'm going to faint.
- I hate who I am.
- I don't have enough faith.
- I'm having a heart attack.
- I can't breath.
- I can't stop shaking.
- I can't panic like this.
- God must not care about me.
- I'm a failure.

One woman sought treatment after she had been unable to sleep for over a week. Her insomnia had been sudden, and after the first few nights of unrest she began to have panic attacks before bedtime. These panic attacks only aggravated her insomnia. She began to think thoughts such as: "If I don't fall asleep soon, I'm going to die. No one can live without sleeping for a week."

The woman had to relearn how to relax and rest at nighttime (and eventually sleep) as well has how to change her thinking patterns. With practice, she successfully managed her anxiety-provoking thoughts.

Listed below are some of the more common physical, emotional, mental, and spiritual causes of anxiety or chronic stress. Remember, most of the time high levels of stress and anxiety are the result of a combination of factors. If you have been experiencing stress and anxiety lately, it may be eye-opening to think about the causes of stress that apply to your life right now. You may be surprised to find what sort of a combination of factors may be contributing to how you feel. Of course, many of the causes of stress and anxiety are unique to an individual and won't be listed here. In addition, you may not know you have some of the following problems without medical attention and counseling.

Physical Causes

- emphysema
- allergic reactions
- asthma
- caffeine use
- diabetes
- inner ear problems (Meniere's disease)
- genetic tendency
- high blood pressure
- medication (OTC & prescription)
- pregnancy
- thyroid problems
- alcoholism
- anemia
- B12 anemia
- depression
- illegal drug use
- abnormal hormone levels
- heart problems
- general illness
- post partum hormonal changes
- premenstrual
- neuropathy

Emotional Causes

- bad living situation
- traumatic events (current or past)
- death of loved one
- financial problems
- moving to a new home or job
- current or past abuse
- chronic stress
- difficult relationship with a family member
- job difficulties
- wayward children
- ill health of family member
- bullying

Mental Causes

- achievement perfectionism
- avoidance thinking
- dwelling on the past
- categorical thinking (B&W thinking)
- constant worrying
- fear of rejection

- incorrect belief system about self
- magnification of problems
- obsessive thinking
- overgeneralization
- over controlling others
- unhealthy thinking patterns
- low frustration levels
- should statements

Spiritual Causes

- belief you are unworthy of God's love
- spiritual perfectionism
- guilt (real or perceived)
- inactivity in spiritual matters
- uncertainty on spiritual matters
- loss of control of one's decisions
- confusion about life's purpose
- fear of spiritual failure
- subjugation (forced or volunteered)
- giving in to temptation or sin
- inability to forgive oneself
- self-blame for others' spirituality

Can't Faith Solve the Problem?

While having faith in Jesus Christ is a powerful ally for peace, it does not often translate into immediate removal of all challenges. God allows us the opportunity to learn line upon line. Faith does not save Latter-day Saints from having even severe anxiety challenges. Nearly 30 percent of the adult population in the United States has had or will have a serious problem with anxiety that requires medical treatment. This figure doesn't include those who suffer from mild anxiety. Latter-day Saints are no different.

Elder Alexander B. Morrison, an emeritus member of the First Quorum of the Seventy, presented a talk on mental health issues. In that talk he explained:

> "I assure you that church leaders are in no way exempt from the burden of mental illness of biological origin, either as victim, or as family member. In the geographic area of every ward and stake there are severely depressed men and women; elderly people with failing memories and reduced intellectual capacities; youth or adults struggling with substance abuse; persons of all ages, both sexes and every walk of life, who exhibit aberrant, even bizarre behavior. Their burdens—and they are many and painful—can only be lifted by love, understanding (both intellectual and spiritual) and acceptance."[12]

Latter-day Saints fall into the trap of thinking that if we are spiritual enough, we will somehow be immune to the stress reaction. This simply isn't so. Chronic anxiety is not a spiritual weakness; it is when the limbic system in the brain is stuck in overdrive.

When we face danger, the limbic system of the brain reacts by increasing the heart rate and blood pressure to get more blood to the muscles, heart and lungs. The body also raises blood sugar levels to provide immediate fuel for the muscles. These physical reactions to stress worked well for ancient civilizations when they faced danger, like an attacking Lamanite warrior. When the warrior was defeated, the body's stress reaction calmed down because of the expended energy.

This same stress reaction, however, is counterproductive when it occurs in a modern situation such as getting cut off in traffic. When dealing with road rage, there is no energy expended. Instead, the limbic system and nervous system reactions build and build and are rarely released unless we purposefully do something to use that energy. Modern-day anxiety often occurs because our "danger" primarily arises from psychological factors rather than physical threats.

When Rachel first went to therapy, she had had moderate anxiety off and on for nearly ten years. One of her first panic attacks came when she was at the LDS Church Distribution center reading a historical account of someone in the 1800s. Being a member of the church her entire life, Rachel had heard much about the early days of the LDS Church, but at this particular moment this pioneer's account of her life set off a panic reaction in Rachel that was so intense she didn't want to return to the distribution center ever again. This feeling of panic returned later when she attended church or even read the scriptures. Then the anxiety started creeping into more of her everyday activities. Since the first panic attack came while Rachel was involved with something spiritual, she incorrectly assumed her problem with anxiety was faith-based.

The truth was Rachel's life had been stressful for some time before her first panic attack at the LDS Church distribution center. Her son was born with a major birth defect, and he had had numerous surgeries even as a young baby. Rachel herself had health problems and had gone through surgery. These physical stresses drained her usual energetic, social and fun-loving self. Rachel may never know the *exact* cause of her first panic attack. However, by looking at all the factors in her life, it becomes clear her panic reaction was a combination of physical and emotional stress that caused her to feel she was not in control of her life.

Different personality types also respond to stress and anxiety differently. The Type A personality is someone who is impatient, hurried, and prompt. These are people who are multi-taskers, overbooked, and clock watchers. Often Type A people walk fast, talk quickly, and eat rapidly. Everyone wants a Type A personality on their team to get things done. Unfortunately, these are also the people who tend to have more anxiety. The Type B personality is someone who is calm, relaxed, and accepting of others. These people find joy in the small, simple things, and they can enjoy down time as much as up time. However, they may be less enthusiastic and not as driven to get things done.

Members of the church have both Type A and Type B personality traits (though typically no one is 100 percent Type A or Type B). It is one of the reasons wards within the LDS Church function so well—we complement each other.

Anxiety Disorders[13]

Some people with anxiety may have an anxiety disorder. There are nine anxiety disorders. Anyone may find they have traits of all the anxiety disorders. This is common. However, for those people who truly suffer from an anxiety disorder, the disorder describes how they feel and act most of the time. Whether you or someone you know has anxiety or an anxiety disorder, the good news is that all levels of anxiety and anxiety disorders are treatable.

Generalized Anxiety Disorder (GAD). GAD is characterized by excessive, unrealistic worry or chronic anxiety that lasts six months or more. Typically the worry may focus on health, money, school, or career. The physical symptoms present include trembling, muscle tension, insomnia, abdominal upsets, dizziness, rapid heartbeat, and irritability. Usually someone with GAD doesn't have panic attacks or phobias.

Obsessive-Compulsive Disorder (OCD). Individuals with OCD are plagued by persistent, recurring thoughts (obsessions) that reflect exaggerated anxiety or fears. The obsessions may cause an individual to perform a ritual or routine to avoid the fear from coming true (compulsions). For example, someone who fears getting sick may ritualistically wash his or her hands to get rid of any germs. By doing the compulsion, the person subconsciously hopes to relieve the anxiety. A religious-related form of OCD is called scrupulosity. Someone with scrupulosity lacks a balanced religious outlook, and they have a fear of having bad or impure thoughts. While the correlation is not clear, a common compulsion for someone with scrupulosity is frequently counting (frontwards or backwards) or even having to touch certain items a number of times.

Panic Disorder. People with panic disorder suffer from sudden and recurring panic attacks that come out of the blue. These attacks make them feel like they are going to die or go crazy. The physical symptoms include heart palpitations, chest pain, sweating, trembling, tingling sensations, and difficulty breathing.

Agoraphobia. Agoraphobia is the fear of having panic attacks in situations or places outside of the home in which it would be difficult to get out of. This causes a person to avoid normal daily activity.

Post-Traumatic Stress Disorder (PTSD). PTSD follows a traumatic event. This event could range from watching a loved one die to being attacked. Symptoms associated with PTSD are reliving the event (flashbacks); avoidance behaviors; emotional detachment; and physical problems like insomnia and difficulty concentrating. These symptoms last more than one month.

Acute Stress Disorder. Acute Stress Disorder lasts less than one month and is defined by exposure to a traumatic event in which a person has been a witness or participant. This event is life threatening, could cause serious injury, or it is a threat to the physical integrity of one's self or others. The person's response involves intense fear, helplessness, flashbacks, avoidance of the situation, and anxiety that lasts for two days to four weeks.

Social Anxiety Disorder (SAD). SAD is when individuals have anxiety about being judged by others. They worry their behavior may cause them embarrassment or ridicule, leading to avoidance of social situations.

Disease-Related Anxiety Disorders. A disease related anxiety disorder is caused by a general medical condition (i.e. lupus, thyroid disease, hypertension, or substance abuse).

Specific phobias. People with specific phobias suffer from an intense reaction to a specific object or situation. Examples might be spiders or water. The way to distinguish between a specific phobia and normal apprehension (like when you see a rattle snake and you experience anxiety) is to check if the level of fear is inappropriate to the situation. Typically people with specific phobias know their fear is irrational.

Recognize that not everyone who has stress has anxiety, and not everyone who experiences anxiety has an anxiety disorder. Those who do have an anxiety disorder may have a mild, moderate, or serious case. The wonderful news is that no matter the level, anxiety is very treatable.

Compounding Physical Illnesses

The first step to managing stress and anxiety is to get a full physical examination. There are several physical conditions that have anxiety as a side effect. For example, low estrogen can be a compounding physical problem. Other possible related illness may be:

- hyperthyroidism
- inner ear disturbances
- premenstrual syndrome
- diabetes
- mononeucleosis
- hypoglycemia
- mitral valve prolapse
- emphysema
- fibromyalgia
- atrial fibrillation

A physical examination will help rule out or pinpoint any compounding physical problems. This will allow for the best possible treatment.

One client came in worried about severe physical symptoms she was experiencing. She wasn't sleeping. She felt irritable and anxious and recently complained of feeling like her skin was crawling. A blood test was recommended to rule out thyroid problems, since this condition ran in her family. The blood test came back positive for hyperactive thyroid.

After treatment for her thyroid condition, she no longer needed counseling services, which saved her time and money.

YOUR OWN STRESS MANAGEMENT PROGRAM

A combination approach to reducing and managing stress and anxiety is one that employs physical, emotional, mental, and spiritual methods together. Remember, it may be hard to pinpoint one thing that is causing all of a person's anxiety. When we approach stress and anxiety from all angles we ensure ourselves better success than if we only approach it on only one front.

In the book, *Behind the Smile*, by LDS entertainer Marie Osmond, she describes how she was able to overcome her post partum depression and anxiety:

> "Once the debilitating physical symptoms of it were under control…to fully recover I found I had to look at my complete state of being, not just physical, but every aspect.
>
> "I tell my children about the balance of our human elements: physical, social, mental, and spiritual, by comparing it to the four legs of a chair. One of the legs on your chair can become weak and break, and, chances are, you will still be able to keep yourself upright by balancing your weight over the other three legs. But if one leg breaks and the other legs of the chair are so weak they just give way, you will find yourself on the floor. I fell so hard it was clear that the legs of my chair had been crumbling beneath me for years. I just didn't know it."[14]

The next few chapters of this book review forty-four techniques to better manage stress in four areas of life—physical, emotional, mental, and spiritual.

Do not read through these chapters and feel you need to do everything at once. Instead, read through these chapters and see what area or areas are your weakest and focus there. Initially, you may want to choose one or two stress-reducing techniques in your weakest area. Work on these techniques for several weeks. Once you feel you have made progress, choose another technique in that area if you still feel it is weak, or move to a different chapter.

If anxiety is currently a troublesome problem in your life, you may want to create your own management plan using these chapters as a guide. Inside a notebook, create four sections. Label them physical, emotional, mental, and spiritual. Then write down one task in each area of health on which you will focus. Be sure to track your progress regularly. Once you have tried a technique, record what you learned, your successes, and how you individualized it for your own situation. Some tasks may be accomplished quickly, others may take longer. An example of a personal stress management plan may look like this:

1. Physical: Learn how to do a muscle tension relaxation exercise. (Chapter Three.)

2. Emotional: Do an emotional assessment and see what emotions I am unsure about expressing. (Chapter Four.)

3. Mental: Identify some of my negative thinking patterns and try to use the "What Will Happen Next" question to get to the core of some of my concerns. (Chapter Five.)

4. Spiritual: Add prayer/meditation to my daily routine each morning. (Chapter Six.)

To improve your mental health, you are going to have to donate some time to it each day. Time is precious for all of us. However, the effort you dedicate now will save you hardships in the future if you let your stress and anxiety grow unchecked. You must decide how much time to give to your management plan each day. About fifteen to twenty minutes a day is a realistic goal, longer if your goals include exercise. As you try different tasks outlined in this book, you will find the ones that work best for you. Once you feel your mental health is strong, these tools you have mastered will be available to you again when you recognize new triggers in your life.

Stress-reducing techniques become anchors to our well-being. I call this the cookie principle. I once worked with a young woman who as a young child had experienced daily trauma at the hands of abusive caregivers. When I asked her how she survived some of the things she experienced, she told me that each night she would go home to her kind grandmother who would help her get ready for bed and give her a freshly baked, warm chocolate chip cookie. During the times of trauma, she would think of the warm sweet chocolate chip cookie she would get that evening. It represented the good thing in her life on which she could always count.

Many children naturally implement this concept into their lives when coping with discomfort. Children look forward to playing, eating sweets, making up fantastical stories in their minds, and seeking comfort from pretend friends. We as adults can also learn to cope with adversity by learning to look forward to the time each day we can reduce stress in our lives. The time you spend on your personal stress management should be healing and beneficial.

Trials Bring Growth

Siddhartha Guatama was a historical religious figure believed to have been born around 563 B.C. He is believed to have been a sage who became Buddha. One of his stories tells of a journey he had hiking with a monk in the bitter-cold of the Himalayas.

On their way up the mountain, Siddhartha and his companion find a man who is seriously injured and cannot walk. Siddhartha tells the monk they must help the man, but the monk tells Siddhartha that because of the cold and their lack of supplies they will die if they try to carry the man. They must first save themselves. Unconvinced, Siddhartha stops to help the man while the monk goes on ahead. Siddhartha continues on his journey, physically exhausted from the chore of carrying the injured man on his back, but he continues out of sheer will power.

As Siddhartha approaches camp, he finds the monk frozen to death in the snow. Siddhartha and the man he saved, however, both make it to camp alive. A universal truth overwhelms him when he realized his life was only spared because of the extra energy he exerted while carrying the man on his back. If he had not had the extra weight, Siddhartha would have perished along with the monk. He concludes that blessed are those persons with challenges, for it is only by working through those challenges that they will arrive at their ultimate desired destination.

I know numerous men and women who through their challenges with stress and anxiety have come to understand Siddhartha's story in a very personal way. As they learn to manage stress and anxiety they find it is the truths they have learned while working through the rough times that have brought them the personal growth they desired.

All of us can grow through trials. I once worked with a very dysfunctional client who was seriously mentally ill and unable to work. He was, by all societal standards, a failure. One night as I was driving home, in my mind's eye a picture unfolded. Life was over and I was standing with a group of people waiting to be judged according to my life's efforts. When my turn came, God asked the group, "Who will testify of the efforts of this woman?"

Only one man came forward to argue my case. It was the seriously mentally ill man I had worked with on earth. Apparently he had already made it to heaven and I was the one who fell short! As he told the crowd of my efforts, I was given leniency. He saved me!

I truly believe our lives are so intertwined that as we help others we end up rescuing ourselves.

CHAPTER THREE—Tools to Manage Physical Symptoms

Paul from the *New Testament* was a prophet who exemplified missionary work. He was also a man who had a physical disability that caused him great anxiety. While no one knows exactly what his physical problem was, some Bible scholars have guessed it was perhaps a stuttering problem or depression. Paul describes his physical challenge as "a thorn in the flesh, the messenger of Satan to buffet me, lest I should be exalted" (2 Cor. 12:6-7).

In 2 Corinthians, Paul reveals that he had asked the Lord several times to take this thorn from him to no avail. Whatever infirmity it was, it stayed with him. He didn't "deserve" the problem because of unrighteousness. It was simply a challenge his physical body had, and something he had to learn to manage.

Paul's shares his insight into physical challenges when he says that his "strength is made perfect in weakness. . . For when I am weak, then am I strong" (2 Cor. 12:9).

A Thorn in the Flesh

Just like Paul, Sally had physical disabilities. She was often anxious due to an inherited mood disorder. Her anxiety symptoms were wide ranging, particularly her physical symptoms. Despite her genetic predisposition to anxiety, she was determined to do her best to care for herself. She studied everything she could, and she worked with her doctor and therapist. She found many things she could do to help improve her anxiety. She monitored her moods daily on a calendar and checked with family members to give her feedback.

She managed her physical symptoms with exercise, nutrition, and using cognitive exercises. After a while, she made a huge difference in how long her anxiety lasted as well as its severity. Her optimism and willingness to accept help helped her evolve into a more compassionate and understanding person. She eventually began to view her mood disorder as more of a stepping stone instead of a road block.

People who experience stress and anxiety haven't "asked for it." On the contrary, like Sally, many are prone to it because of a genetic tendency. However, once we recognize our weakness in this area, it is our challenge (and opportunity) to learn how we can grow from it.

It's in the Genes

Biologically speaking, much of what goes on inside the body of someone with chronic stress and anxiety is physical in nature. In the early 20th century, an endocrinologist named Hans Selye coined the term "stress response." Using rats, Dr. Selye studied how rats responded differently to danger. Later, Dr. Selye studied the human stress response, which is defined as the human body's physical reactions, both visible and unseen, to a perceived threat. He concluded everyone has a stress response. However, in some people that stress response turns chronic, or elevates into anxiety. The reason for this is often found within a person's physical makeup.

As discussed in Chapter Two, a stress reaction involves an outpouring of adrenaline and cortisol into the bloodstream. Imagine waking up in the middle of the night to the sound of your smoke alarm beeping. You sniff the air. . . and smell smoke! Instantly your body shoots adrenaline and cortisol into your blood. You go from sleeping to wide awake in seconds. As you bolt from your bed, let's take a quick look at what is happening inside your body. 1) Muscles are tense, ready for action. 2) Blood is rushing to the survival part of the brain to help stimulate action. 3) Your heart is beating faster to push blood more quickly to the muscles and brain. 4) Breathing speeds up to supply more oxygen for the increase in blood circulation. 5) The cognitive or higher order parts of the brain shut down, along with the speech center. All of these reactions would enable you, if the fire was real, to respond quickly and accurately to save your life.

Someone with chronic stress or anxiety may have this intense of a stress/panic response on a regular basis with no obvious threat to physical safety. But just because there is no real threat doesn't mean the physical reactions to stress and anxiety aren't real. In fact, a panic attack causes the fastest and most complex reaction known within the human body. It alters the function of the eyes, several major glands, brain, heart, lungs, stomach, intestines, pancreas, kidneys, bladder, and the major muscle groups.

The stress response is a built-in survival function that, at times, can go awry. This is not uncommon in the body. Take for instance acne and allergies. Acne is the result of the endocrine (hormone) system malfunctioning and producing extra oils. Allergies are a condition where the immune system becomes confused and reacts to everyday things like dust and grass.

The Limbic/Nervous System Gone Awry

Why does the nervous system in some people overact and not in others? Everyone is different, so there are many possibilities. An existing health condition may compromise the way the limbic system or nervous system functions. Diabetes, heart disease, menopause, and other physical conditions may be at the root of stress and anxiety. One study showed that 57 percent of women who have active heart disease suffer from anxiety and depression.[15]

Others who experience chronic stress and anxiety may have an imbalance of serotonin and possibly other chemicals found in the brain. For example, researchers at the National Institute of Mental Health reported key components of a chemical messenger that regulates emotion were lacking in the brains of people with a panic disorder. By doing brain scans, scientists found there are one-third less receptors (or receivers) of serotonin in three different areas of the brain in people with a panic disorder.[16] These findings prove what scientists have believed for several decades. If a person has a lower number of serotonin receptors, he or she is more likely to overreact to stress.

Drug abuse can also alter serotonin levels. Chronic use of stimulants, pain killers, narcotics, and alcohol can reduce serotonin levels and create chronic anxiety. Drugs destroy receptor sites in the brain, creating a permanent deficiency in neurotransmitters such as serotonin. "Drug burn out" refers to permanently damaging brain neurons, which then creates permanent anxiety and depression in drug users.

Another way in which the limbic and nervous system may go awry is from growing a high number of dendrites in the brain. Dendrites are an extension of brain neurons that accept or receive messages. They are complex in nature, and we don't understand everything about them. What we do know, however, is that the more dendrites we have, the more messages we receive. If someone has an average number of dendrites and the brain releases stress-related chemicals, a normal number of those chemicals are received. This results in a typical "stress reaction."

Now let's suppose a person has an increased number of dendrites. When his or her body releases the same amount of stress-related chemicals, a larger number of those chemicals will be received by the dendrites. In other words, a normal stress response is amplified by the number of dendrites receiving the signal. This is how the same stressor can cause such a different reaction in different people.

There are two ways an individual may grow an increased number of dendrites. The first way is genetic. It's like inheriting blond hair or freckles. A parent's DNA may pass on the coding for extra dendrites.

Allen E. Bergin, former professor of psychology at BYU, made an interesting point concerning inherited physical weakness. He said:

> "We live in a fallen world, in which environment, biology, or both may work against mental health and normal conduct. The children of Adam are natural heirs to the ills of mortality; but through Christ's Atonement they are all redeemed from the curse of this fallen state. Of course, this does not mean that those who have the capacity to change are justified in doing nothing about the problems passed on to them, rationalizing that they will not be held accountable for their actions."[17]

The second way a person may grow large numbers of dendrites is by being exposed in childhood to traumatic experiences. The neurons in a child's brain continue to grow new dendrites until about the age of nine or ten. A child who is abused, neglected, or who experiences repeated traumatic experiences before this age will grow an increased number of dendrites. This explains why a significant percent of abused children grow up to be adults with anxiety and depression. Past abuse and trauma should be dealt with, and worked through, but it need not become a crutch for hopelessness.

Emeritus member of the First Quorum of the Seventy Alexander B. Morrison explains:

> "Ascribing blame for mental illness causes unnecessary suffering for all concerned and takes time and energy which would be better used to increase understanding of what actually is happening—to get a complete assessment and proper diagnosis of the illness involved, understand the causations—often ultimately, changes in brain chemistry—get proper medication which will help control the disorder by reversing those chemical changes and learn behavioral and cognitive techniques that are part of the healing process."[18]

Since the physical basis of stress and anxiety is biologically based, each person must learn techniques to counteract the body's physical response to stress and anxiety. Each of the techniques discussed in this chapter helps boost brain chemicals (i.e. neurotransmitters such as serotonin), which are important in regulating stress and anxiety.

Physical Management Techniques:

1. Eat Correctly

There are several ways what you eat affects how you feel. Stable blood sugar levels promote calmness, energy, and emotional stability. On the other hand, unstable blood sugar promotes anxiety, fatigue, and feeling like you are on an emotional rollercoaster. If you are not a diabetic or hypoglycemic (and sometimes even if you are) you can better stabilize blood sugar levels by eating more frequent meals with balanced amounts of protein and carbohydrates. Since refined carbohydrates (such as refined sugar, flour, rice, and pasta) quickly raise blood sugar levels, it is best to stick with complex carbohydrates such as whole wheat bread, brown rice, beans, oatmeal, and complex fruits and vegetables.

Eating protein, low-fat dairy, or soybeans also helps in managing stress and anxiety. In World War II, the U.S. military found that feeding bomber pilots frequent servings of protein during their flights helped them remain calm and alert even under intense pressure.

Eating correctly can also positively affect beta-endorphins, a brain chemical closely related to serotonin. Beta-endorphins are chemicals that aid in pain control and in feeling happy and relaxed.

Some things to avoid are: caffeinated drinks, chocolate, and the herb guarana, all of which contain caffeine and stimulate the nervous system. Another herb to stay away from is ephedra (also called ma-huang).

Some over-the-counter medications can trigger anxiety. Many over-the-counter decongestants can stimulate the nervous system and promote anxiety symptoms. There are also numerous prescription medications that have nervousness as a possible side effect. Check with your doctor if you have a question about a prescription medication you are taking.

2. Consider Natural Supplements

There has been a lot written about natural supplements. It seems most people adhere to one of two camps: they are either for them or against them. For those interested in trying natural supplements, recognize that while they may help, rarely do they produce a complete solution. They often must be used in combination with other techniques.

Should a person use supplements or something stronger? This question needs to be discussed with a health care professional. It comes down to one question: Are you satisfied with your quality of life using milder methods to manage anxiety? Be honest with yourself. People diagnosed with mild diabetes can often manage their blood sugar levels without insulin through diet and exercise. However, if a diabetic's quality of life becomes too unpredictable and uncomfortable using these methods, a physician will place the person on medication. It is similar with medication to manage mental health. Some people manage anxiety using natural techniques that don't include medication. On the other hand, some need the medication (at least for a period of time) as much as a severe diabetic needs insulin.

For those against supplements, you may want to look at the many scientific studies reporting positive results achieved with natural supplements.[19,20] The effects of supplements are typically subtle and only manifest themselves after an extended period of time.

One of the first things I ask my clients who come to me with stress and anxiety is, "How much calcium and magnesium are you taking?" These two minerals are very important to the body in promoting a healthy nervous system. Deficiencies in other vitamins, amino acids, and fatty acids can also contribute to an agitated nervous system.

The following is a list (in alphabetical order) of some vitamins, minerals, and herbs that have been used by nutritionists to help manage stress and anxiety. Check with your doctor before using supplements to avoid any negative interactions.

Avena Satina (oats). Avena satina is believed to help soothe the nervous system and possibly help lower anxiety levels and cholesterol.

Calcium. Calcium is used in the body in the sheathing around the nerves. By increasing calcium, you may over time, build up this sheath and strengthen the nerves. Calcium also helps with muscle twitching.

Chamomile. Chamomile is used as an herbal tea, and it is believed to promote relaxation and calm the nervous system.

DHEA. DHEA is an over-the-counter hormone supplement used to help with anxiety from hormone imbalance. Many nutritionists believe you should only take this with the consent of your doctor, and that first you should have your hormone levels tested.

Evening Primrose Oil – This supplement has been shown to act as a natural anti-inflammatory that may calm nerves.

Kava Kava. Kava has been used anciently and modernly in the reduction of stress and anxiety. There has been a lot of research on this herb. Some studies show it may be effective in lowering anxiety levels. However, the FDA has put out a warning because it may compromise the health of the liver.

Licorice Root. Licorice root has been used by nutritionists to help regulate the adrenal glands that create cortisol and adrenaline.

Magnesium. When cortisol levels in the body are high (as in the case of chronic stress and anxiety), the body tends to excrete more magnesium in the urine, leaving the body low on this important mineral. Magnesium builds up the nerves, and helps reduce muscle tension.

Manganese. Manganese is a trace mineral that is low in people experiencing stress and anxiety. Boosting manganese may be one way to lower stress.

Melatonin. Melatonin is an over-the-counter supplement that may help promote restfulness and sleep. This supplement may be useful for people with stress and anxiety who are also experiencing insomnia.

Miscellaneous Herbs. Other herbs that have been used to promote calmness and lower stress levels are Passionflower, Asian Ginseng, Hops, and Gotu Kola.

Omega 3 & 6 Fatty Acids. Omega 3 and Omega 6 fatty acids are considered essential fatty acids, which means that they are essential to human health but cannot be manufactured by the body. It is important to maintain an appropriate balance of Omega 3 and Omega 6 since these two substances work together to promote health, particularly brain function because the brain is made up of 70 percent fatty acids. Omegas 3 and 6 have been shown to help with depression and anxiety.

Pantothenic Acid. Pantothenic acid may help regulate the adrenal gland, which produces adrenaline and cortisol.

Potassium. Potassium is a mineral that helps reduce muscle cramping and twitching, both of which are common symptoms in someone with stress and anxiety.

Siberian Ginseng. Siberian ginseng has a long list of benefits according to many nutritionists. One of its believed functions is lowering stress and promoting chemical balance. It may also increase energy levels.

Soy. Soy may help reduce anxiety levels that are associated with menopause or other hormone imbalances.

Thiamine. Thiamine may be useful in lowering high levels of cortisol in the body.

Valerian Root. Valerian root has been used as a natural sleep aid for many years by different cultures. It is believed to relax the central nervous system, promote feelings of calm, and decrease levels of anxiety and stress.

Vitamin B-Complex. B-complex vitamins are rapidly used up in the body. They are useful in many body functions, including managing stress and anxiety.

Vitamin C. Vitamin C is believed to boost the immune system and support the adrenal glands.

Zinc. Zinc is another trace mineral that is low in someone with stress and anxiety.

3. Assess the Need for Medication

Statistics show that currently there are 20 million people with moderate to severe anxiety in the United States. It is believed that approximately half of those people treat their anxiety with alcohol.

Treating anxiety with alcohol is widely accepted in our society. One LDS client was astounded when, as a pregnant woman, she called her doctor for help with anxiety-related insomnia. Her doctor told her that regardless of her pregnancy or religion, a glass of wine before bedtime would help her insomnia. While it is true that in the beginning alcohol may be effective in masking anxiety, after a short while it backfires and actually increases anxiety. It is much wiser to use a prescription medication that is monitored by a doctor rather than self-medicate with alcohol or illegal drugs.

As with anything in life, there are differing opinions in regard to medication. On the two extremes, some people want to take medication after one bad day. Others believe medication is a sign of character weakness or that they are not exerting faith in themselves or God if they resort to medication.

The decision of whether or not to use medication depends on the level of anxiety, the type of anxiety, a person's comfort zone with anxiety, the length of anxiety, and the other types of treatment being used. All of these factors need to be discussed with a doctor. Alexander B. Morrison, emeritus member of the Quorum of the Seventy explains:

> "Just as we would not hesitate to consult a physician about medical problems such as cancer, heart disease, or diabetes, we should not hesitate to obtain medical and other appropriate professional assistance in dealing with mental illness... We don't say to persons with heart disease or cancer, 'just grow up and get over it.' Neither should we treat the mentally ill in such an uncompassionate and unhelpful way.... During the past forty years numerous medications, effective against one or more forms of mental illness, have been developed.... These potent products have proven of inestimable worth to millions. Not that they are perfect, or work effectively and specifically in every instance... (However) research on brain chemistry and physiology, and on the nature, location and effects on mental and physical function of chemical neurotransmitters in the brain, is speeding the day when physicians will have available effective drugs which are specific in correcting the biochemical lesion or lesions concerned. I have no doubt that such advances, which we are already beginning to see, will result in striking advances in the therapy of mental illness over the next decade."[21]

The LDS Church has never equated taking medication with unfaithfulness, sin, or weakness of character. One the contrary, even since the earliest days of the restoration, leaders in the LDS Church have encouraged members to do all within their available resources to take care of themselves. Take for instance the well-known quote by Brigham Young:

> "If we are sick, and ask the Lord to heal us, and to do all for us that is necessary to be done, according to my understanding of the Gospel of salvation, I might as well ask the Lord to cause my wheat and corn to grow, without my plowing the ground and casting in the seed. It appears consistent to me to apply every remedy that comes within the range of my knowledge, and to ask my Father in Heaven, in the name of Jesus Christ, to sanctify that application to the healing of my body.
>
> "But suppose we were traveling in the mountains, … and one or two were taken sick, without anything in the world in the shape of healing medicine within our reach, what should we do? According to my faith, ask the Lord Almighty to … heal the sick. This is our privilege, when so situated that we cannot get anything to help ourselves. Then the Lord and his servants can do all. But it is my duty to do, when I have it in my power."[22]

Elder Richard G. Scott, of the Quorum of the Twelve, had this to say to full-time LDS missionaries in conference about medication, particularly medication that is used in maintaining mental well-being:

> "If you have emotional challenges that can be stabilized to meet the rigors of a full-time mission, you can be called. It is vital that you continue to use your medication during your mission, or until competent medical authority counsels otherwise. Recognize that emotional and physical challenges are alike. One needs to do all that is possible to improve the situation, then learn to live within the remaining bounds. God uses challenges that we may grow by conquering them."[23]

Once medication is started, it must be taken daily and monitored by a medical doctor or psychiatrist. It is recommended that certain medications for anxiety or depression be used for at least six to twelve months to be beneficial. In patients with chronic anxiety, medication may be used for longer periods of time and in conjunction with therapy.

There are different types of medication used to treat chronic stress and anxiety. The following is a brief overview of some of the common medications used for anxiety.

<u>Selective Serotonin Reuptake Inhibitors (SSRIs)</u>

SSRI drugs are considered modern anti-depressant drugs often used for anxiety. They are non-addicting because they take two to four weeks before the benefits are felt. Each SSRI drug has its own benefits, dosage, and possible side effects, though side effects for most people are minimal. The medication should be taken in the morning.

- Prozac (fluoxetine)
- Zoloft (sertraline)
- Paxil (paroxetine)
- Lexapro (escitalopram oxalate)

- Luvox (fluvoxamine maleate) often used for treatment of OCD
- Celexa (citalopram)

Selective Serotonin and Norephinephrine Reuptake Inhibitor (SSNRI)

SSNRIs are closely associated to SSRIs, but they increase two chemicals, serotonin and norephinephrine, naturally found in the brain and in the spinal cord. The names of these drugs are:

- Cymbalta (duloxetine)
- Effexor (venlafaxine)
- Serzone (nefazodone)

TCAs (Tricyclic Anti-Depressants)

Tricyclic antidepressants are considered older antidepressants. They were used widely in the 60s, 70s, and 80s. They affect norepinephrine and serotonin. TCAs are as effective as the newer antidepressants, but they typically have more side effects than the SSRIs.

- Elavil
- Tofranil
- Aventyl
- Amitriplyline
- Pamelor
- Vivactil

Other Anti-depressant Medication used for Anxiety

- Remeron – more sedating medication that adjusts the brain's levels of norepinephrine and serotonin.
- Wellbutrin – an anti-depressant that is chemically different than the tricyclics, SSRIs, and other medication.

Benzodiazepines

These medications are only prescribed for brief periods of time because a person taking benzodiazepines for weeks or months may a develop tolerance for and dependence on these drugs. Abuse and withdrawal reactions are also possible. The effects from these medications are felt immediately.

- Lorazepam (Ativan)
- Klonipin
- Diazepam (Valium)
- Alprazolam (Xanax)
- Serax

Other Short-term Anti-anxiety Medications

These drugs should only be used on a short-term basis because they are habit forming and have strong side effects.

- Hydroxyzine hydrochloride (Atarax)
- Meprobamate (Equanil)
- Droperidol (Inapsine)
- Chlormezanone (Trancopal)
- Hydroxyzine pamoate (Vistaril)

4. Perform Abdominal (Diaphragmatic) Breathing

Abdominal breathing is an easy and effective way to quickly lower stress and anxiety. When using abdominal breathing, purposely breathe using your diaphragm muscles. Studies have shown actual differences in the breathing patterns of stressed, anxious, and shy people versus people who are relaxed. The first group breathes in a shallow fashion from their chest, while those in the relaxed group breathe more slowly, deeply, and from their abdomen. The good news is that breathing is one involuntary body function you can control.

When in a stressful or anxious situation, you can reduce the stress you feel by changing your breathing patterns. It is also possible to practice abdominal breathing on a regular basis to retrain yourself to breathe more deeply and from your abdomen. This may help in preventing future overactive stress responses in the body. Some of the physical reactions of abdominal breathing are:

- Improved mental focus
- a relaxation response
- stimulation of the parasympathetic nervous system that promotes calmness

Abdominal Breathing Exercise

1. Put one hand on your abdomen right beneath your rib cage.
2. Breathe slowly and deeply in through your nose and send the air as low as you can into your lungs. If you're breathing from your abdomen, your hand should actually rise. The upper chest only moves slightly when you breathe from your diaphragm and abdomen.
3. After you have taken a full, deep breath, hold it in until you notice a little discomfort (usually counting slowly to five does it). Then exhale slowly through your mouth with a sigh (again counting to five in your head may help you do it gradually). It helps to try and relax your whole body as you exhale. This may take some visualization that we will discuss later. You may also try and make your muscles go limp.

4. Do five abdominal breaths to begin. Keep the breathing smooth and regular, try not to do shallow breaths in between. It will go something like this: Slowly inhale through the nose. Hold your breath five counts. Slowly exhale through mouth with a sigh while you count inside your head to five. Relax muscles. Pause. Repeat the process three more times.
5. You can try doing three sets of five abdominal breaths several times a day as a sort of daily exercise.
6. Please note, if you start to feel light-headed while practicing this exercise, stop for thirty seconds and then start again.

5. Learn Muscle Relaxation

Many people with stress and anxiety don't notice how tense their muscles are until their muscles begin cramping, having spasms, or twitching. By reducing muscle tension, you will bring relief to your muscles and to your mind.

One of the first physicians to teach muscle relaxation was Dr. Edmund Jacobson from Chicago. In 1929 he wrote a book which he called *Progressive Relaxation* wherein he explained that the body responds to anxious thoughts with muscle tension. This muscle tension triggers more anxious thoughts, which begins a cycle of anxiety. He believed if you could stop muscle tension, you could break the stress cycle. He wrote, "An anxious mind cannot exist in a relaxed body."[24]

Some common areas of muscle tension are the eye muscles, the jaw area, neck, shoulders, back, and stomach. Of course, any muscle may be tense from stress and anxiety. The idea behind progressive muscle relaxation is to purposely tense the muscles for ten seconds in common areas of tension, and then release the muscle, which forces the once-tense muscle to relax. Muscle relaxation can be used in three different ways to reduce stress or anxiety.

First, before an obvious stress trigger such as a performance or a job interview, take a few minutes and do some progressive muscle relaxation. Consider it part of your preparation for the big event.

Another time to use progressive muscle relaxation is when you experience unexpected anxiety or stress, such as if you have a sudden panic attack. The action of tensing and relaxing the muscles in your body will help the body use up adrenaline more quickly, and it will help get your mind thinking of something else. In this situation, continue the muscle tensing and relaxing until the panic goes away.

The third way to use progressive muscle relaxation is to do it regularly each day for five to ten minutes (as part of an exercise routine) to help your mind learn to recognize muscle tension. Chronic muscle tension is a red flag to someone with chronic stress. It tells you anxiety is building and a change in routine may be necessary. Through the regular practice of progressive muscle relaxation, you will be able to recognize muscle tension and prevent major anxiety by noticing symptoms before they become overwhelming. Many of my clients report these exercises as being what has helped the most in bringing their anxiety and panic attacks under control.

Progressive Muscle Relaxation Exercise

To begin, try to do muscle relaxation in a quiet place, alone, with no distractions. Take your shoes off, loosen your clothing, and get comfortable in a chair. I like to begin at the top (the head) and move down the body. Try and focus your mind on the muscle group you are targeting. It's important to feel the tension and the fatigue.

1. Grimace your mouth outward, tensing the muscles all the way down into the neck. Hold for ten seconds. Release and feel your face muscles relax. Take an abdominal breath and hold for five seconds. Release. If needed, take a few more abdominal breaths before starting the next muscle group.

2. Raise your eyebrows, open your eyes wide, and extend your tongue as far as it can go. (Yes, you will look strange.) Hold for ten seconds. Release and feel your jaw and eye muscles relax. Take an abdominal breath and hold for five seconds. Release. If needed, take a few more breaths before starting the next muscle group.

3. Take your shoulders and bring them up to your ears as high as they will go. Hold for ten seconds. Release and feel your neck muscles relax. Take an abdominal breath and hold for five seconds. Release. If needed, take a few more abdominal breaths before starting the next muscle group.

4. Clench your left and right fists. Bend your elbows and pull your fists up to your shoulders. Then push your clenched fists and elbows toward your back, tensing your back muscles. Hold for ten seconds. Release and feel your hand, arm, shoulder, and back muscles relax. Take an abdominal breath and hold for five seconds. Release. If needed, take a few more abdominal breaths before starting the next muscle group.

5. Focus on the abdominal muscles found in the center of your stomach right below your rib cage. Pull these muscles inside your body toward your back. Hold for ten seconds. Release and feel your stomach muscles relax. Take an abdominal breath and hold for five seconds. Release. If needed, take a few more abdominal breaths before starting the next muscle group.

6. Point your toes, flex your calves, tighten your thighs, and squeeze your buttocks together. Hold for twenty seconds (these larger muscles need to be tensed for a longer time for the same effect.) Shaking is normal. Release and feel the muscles in the lower half of your body relax. Take an abdominal breath and hold for five seconds. Release. If needed, take a few more abdominal breaths.

Repeat the exercise until your muscles are fatigued, relaxed, and the anxiety has passed. You can add different muscles to this exercise if you like, or you may separate the muscle groups into smaller bundles. For example, just squeeze your buttocks together for twenty seconds and then relax. Then tighten the thigh muscles, and so on.

During muscle relaxation, some people choose a word or a sound on which to focus called a mantra.) Something like "um" or "relax" may work, or you can choose your own. Besides releasing adrenaline from the muscles, progressive muscle relaxation may help invoke a relaxation response, which is when the sympathetic nervous system is stimulated by rhythmical breathing and motion.

6. Exercise

Regular exercise is a great way to change brain chemistry, promote calmness, and manage stress. Some people with anxiety respond incredibly well to physical exercise. To get the best effects, you should do it every day for at least thirty to sixty minutes. One woman had anxiety in connection with an eating disorder. She tried various types of treatments (including medication) before discovering exercise. When she regularly exercised as part of her treatment, she found her ability to manage her anxiety and eating disorder was significantly increased.

Ninety percent of the studies report that exercise is an anti-anxiety (and anti-depressant) activity. So how does it work? Exercise does several things in the body. After about thirty minutes of moderate exercise the body releases increased levels of beta-endorphins, a brain chemical related to serotonin that is linked to a feeling of well being. The increase in beta-endorphins continues, even after the exercise stops. Exercise also increases the availability of central neurotransmitters in the brain, which is beneficial in regulating brain chemistry. From a psychological standpoint, exercising gives a sense of control and a feeling of self mastery.

People always ask me what type of exercise is the best. The answer is simply whatever kind you like and will do. One study found that leisure-time physical activities (no matter at what level of aerobic exertion) were found to be equally effective in preventing stress and anxiety.[25] It is not necessary to exhaust your body while exercising. In fact, moderation is preferred.

Types of Different Exercises

Aerobics	Biking
Dancing	Hiking
Jogging	Karate
Pilates	Power yoga
Rock climbing	Rowing
Running	Skiing
Swimming	Tennis
Walking	Water aerobics
Wogging	

7. Sleep

So often, those who have a tendency toward elevated stress and anxiety are the very same people who push themselves to the limit, particularly when it comes to getting enough sleep. The stress-prone person will often give up a few hours (or more) of sleep to get more accomplished in a day. This habit may eventually backfire. During deep sleep, the brain has time to produce more of the brain chemicals needed for the next day.

Serotonin is a by-product of deep sleep (or slow-wave sleep). Conversely, when we are in REM (Rapid Eye Movement) or light dream sleep, our bodies stop the production of serotonin. Additionally, during deep sleep the body repairs itself and produces the Growth Hormone (especially in children). We cycle in and out of deep sleep during the sleep cycle.

When you deprive yourself of sleep on a regular basis, you may create a chemical imbalance. You produce less neurotransmitters needed for concentration and normal brain functioning. Your body can't repair organs and muscles so it may experience injury more easily. It doesn't matter how intelligent, spiritual, or successful you are. Taking care of your body means getting the rest it needs. The following is a true story from a man who experienced his first panic attack after depriving himself of sleep for an extended period of time:

> *My first experience with a panic attack occurred as a result of several factors all combining together. The actual incident happened in the fall, which is significant because the fall season has always presented a bit of a crisis to me. Every spring I outline all of the projects that I wanted to accomplish with my spare time. The list of projects was always unachievable. Fall represented a judgment time, when I realized all of the things I didn't get done.*
>
> *This particular fall was no exception. In the spring I had been promoted to general manager. I was excited about the opportunity, but also felt unprepared and inadequate. At the same time I was in the middle of selling the home and relocating to another area of town. In order to increase the resale value of our home, I was converting the basement of our house into an apartment, and I was doing all of the work myself. In addition, I was volunteering a lot of my time at my church.*

Following the urgings from the real estate agent, we placed the house on the market before the basement was completed. The house sold, sight unseen, three days after the listing was published. Wanting to facilitate the sale of the home, I unrealistically committed to have the basement apartment done in a month. I continued on with the basement and felt excited at first, working well into the evenings. I soon realized I had not been realistic with the completion date, and I doubted my ability to complete the project on time. But I felt I had to finish it.

Every night, right after my day job, I would arrived at the home and begin working. My answer to the problem was that I would have to work longer hours. I began working through the night on the project, telling my wife that she would see me when she saw me. I remember one particular evening when I had gotten into a work grove, getting so much accomplished, when I looked out the window and realized it was day. I had worked the entire night away and it was time to go back to work at my day job.

Getting closer to my deadline, it still appeared I wouldn't be done on time. That is when the panic attack happened. I was thinking how I wasn't going to make my deadline, when I was filled with complete terror. I was in the middle of the basement project and there was no danger was present when I became physically and emotionally paralyzed. I broke out in a sweat, my heart was racing, and I couldn't think rationally. I felt trapped, stuck, and hopeless, like there was no way out and that something terrible was going to happen to me and my family.

This man had physically pushed his body to the extreme, and his body, mind, and emotions were overwhelmed, giving him panic when there was no real impending terror. Among other things, he learned he had to give his body the rest it needed in order for him to stay healthy. By neglecting physical needs, our bodies may be pushed into panic mode.

Insomnia

A common symptom of stress and anxiety is insomnia. Once a person's level of adrenaline and cortisol are too high, he or she may have a hard time falling asleep or staying asleep. This inability to sleep feeds stress, and nighttime becomes a time of panic instead of a time of relaxation and rejuvenation. Insomnia is described as either the inability to fall asleep or premature waking in the night with the inability to go back to sleep.

For someone who has anxiety-related insomnia, sleep is not the goal. Instead, nighttime should be approached as a time of relaxation, meditation, and calm activities that can also produce an increase in needed brain chemicals, even without deep sleep. Once adrenaline and cortisol levels are decreased, insomnia will lift and the ability to fall into a deep sleep will return.

Each year 60 million Americans deal with insomnia—four in every ten women and three in every ten men. The National Sleep Foundation reports that 35 percent of all adults experience symptoms of insomnia every night, while 58 percent report symptoms at least a few nights a week.

Short-term insomnia is usually caused by immediate stress and long-term insomnia may be the result of chronic anxiety or depression.

There may be other factors involved as well such as medication, pain, hormones, caffeine consumption, etc. Another common cause of insomnia is the way people respond to their inability to sleep. After not sleeping well for several days, some people respond by becoming worried, frustrated, or depressed. This leads to increased stress at bedtime, which further interferes with sleep.

Studies show that therapy and other non-drug techniques are more effective than sleeping pills in treating chronic insomnia.[26] Unfortunately, sleeping pills are the most frequent treatment. In most cases, however, once the sleeping pills are discontinued the sleep problems return. In this section we will discuss ways to deal with insomnia without taking sleeping pills.

To begin, it may be useful to ask yourself a few questions to evaluate where or when the problem with insomnia started.

1. When did the problem begin?
2. Is the sleep problem mostly about getting to sleep, staying asleep, or both?
3. Did the insomnia start with any medical problem or stressful life event?
4. Did the insomnia start with any other circumstance, such as starting or stopping a prescription or over-the-counter medication?
5. Do I sleep O.K. in other environments such as in a hotel, hospital, or even another room in my house?

Your answers to these questions may help you better understand what is fueling your insomnia.

Ease Back into Sleep

Approximately four out of ten people with insomnia medicate themselves to get to sleep. One of the most common substances used is alcohol. Others use both non-prescription and/or prescription sleep aids. In the long run, alcohol and sleep aids aren't the solution. In fact, sleeps aids have been shown to interfere with deep sleep, and they can even increase anxiety in some people.

A long-term solution is to learn to ease back into sleep. This begins by doing those things during the day that promote good mental health such as exercise and muscle relaxation. You should also avoid taking naps. At night, go to bed at your normal time. If sleep doesn't come within 20 minutes get up and do a restful activity. Things like crocheting, whittling, looming a hat, reading (no mystery novels), giving yourself a pedicure, folding laundry, or taking a bath. After your first activity is finished, start a new one that is even more restful—things such as listening to a book on tape (not a suspenseful book), relaxed reading, listening to music, or sipping chamomile tea. After that activity, begin another one that is even more restful. Try things such as meditation, visualization (floating in nothingness), rocking in a chair, or watching the flames in a gas fireplace. Finally, lie down and allow yourself the opportunity to fall asleep again. If sleep doesn't come after 20 minutes, start the process over.

Each time you take your activity down a level, you prepare your body for sleep. By keeping activities restful, you are also promoting relaxation. If you can't sleep, that's okay. Being restful and relaxed are the next best things to sleep. Be sure to get up at the same time you would normally. This will help your body develop a normal sleep pattern, even though you aren't sleeping, just resting.

By staying in bed and panicking over the fact that you can't sleep, a person create negative associations with the bed, bedroom, or sleep in general. Sometimes, when negative associations with sleep are created, it triggers unconscious expectations of failure, disappointment, shame, and frustration.

The following list contains suggestions that may help in easing yourself back into sleep. Find which ones work best for you.

- A nice cool temperature is typically the best for getting to sleep. Don't keep the bedroom too warm.
- After being in bed for 20 minutes, get up and do something else relaxing.
- Don't exercise vigorously too close to bedtime.
- Don't take long naps during the day.
- Don't watch T.V. late at night, especially "thrillers" or shows with upsetting themes.
- Drink a warm glass of milk before bedtime. Milk contains tryptophan, an amino acid that helps induce sleep.
- Exercise every day.
- Keep clocks and other time cues away from your bed.
- Learn about any medications you may be taking. Things such as alcohol, caffeine, bronchodilators, beta blockers, steroids (prednisone/cortisone), calcium blockers, over-the-counter decongestants and cold remedies, dilantin, and thyroid medication may cause or contribute to insomnia.
- Relax before bedtime. Take a bath or read (for pleasure).
- Set a schedule for going to sleep and waking up and stick to it.

- Set aside a period of time (ten minutes) and “get out” all of your thoughts by writing them down on a paper. Some people find keeping a pad and pencil by their bedside is helpful.
- Try using background noise (i.e. a fan, vaporizer, humidifier, or other mechanical device).
- Try using a relaxing natural supplement such as chamomile tea, valerian root, or melatonin. (See the section on natural supplements.)
- Use your bed only for sleeping. Don’t read, watch television, or eat in bed.
- Wake up with the sun or use very bright lights in the morning. An hour of sunlight exposure in the morning can help you sleep better at night.

8. Soak up Sunlight

It’s free, it feels good, and it may be just what you need to calm an overactive nervous system. Sunlight has been shown in many studies to help stimulate the production of important brain chemicals and invoke mental well- being.

For example, a study done in Melbourne, Australia, which appeared in *The Lancet*, showed that sunlight directly influences the body’s production of serotonin. In the study, blood samples were taken from one hundered and one healthy men during each of the four seasons and compared with various weather factors, such as temperature, rainfall, hours of bright sunlight the men experienced, and atmospheric pressure.[27] Researchers found that regardless of the season, the rate of serotonin production in the brain was directly related to the men’s exposure to bright sunlight.

People who are prone to chronic stress and anxiety should get at least 30 minutes and up to three hours of sunlight a day. The best way to do this is to actually be outside. The use of sunscreen is important. If that is not possible, indoor, full spectrum lights at 10,000 LUX in intensity can be used. Light boxes are available for those with Seasonal Affective Disorder, a condition that surfaces during the winter when sunlight hours are limited.

9. Enjoy Physical Touch

For some people, physical touch initiates a release of beta-endorphins, the same healthy brain chemicals that exercise releases. This is why a hug from a good friend may be just the thing to brighten your day, or why a back rub from a spouse has the ability to calm you down. Even having a shower gives the body a sensation of physical touch and may increase beta-endorphin production.

In one study, a group of adults were given a chair massage two times a week for five weeks. A control group simply relaxed in chair during this same time. At the end of five weeks, the group that received massages had reduced stress, lower cortisol levels in their saliva, and increased speed and accuracy on math tests.[28]

Comforting touch also creates serotonin in the brain. In studies of infants in orphanages, it was found that babies who were held and touched frequently thrived, whereas babies who received little touch or physical stimulation often didn't.[29]

A study on eating disorders showed that women who suffered from anorexia (a condition strongly tied to anxiety) had lower anxiety symptoms after massage therapy was introduced into their treatment. Women in the control group who did not have the massage therapy showed less improvement in anxiety symptoms.[30]

The power of positive touch is enormous. It is no wonder that when the elderly lose a spouse their life expectancy is reduced. Men live longer lives when they are married. Children are better adjusted when they come from homes where they received a high amount of physical touch and nurturing, especially as an infant. There is a healing power in nurturing touch.

Simple Types of Physical Touch that May Relieve Stress

- Massage
- Hugs
- Back rubs
- Foot massages
- Hand massages
- Facial
- Shower
- Bath
- Getting a haircut

10. Experiment with Eye Movement

In the middle of a stressful situation, our eyes tend to focus on one object, for example a barking dog. This physical reaction of focusing our field of vision increases the body's reaction to the stressor.

Researchers have been studying Eye Movement Desensitization Response or EMDR. It is a technique that some people use to manage stress and anxiety. It is helpful in a public situation when it would be awkward to do a progressive muscle relaxation.

One form of eye movement works by simply moving your eyes, without moving your head, from the left all the way to the right, and then back again to the left again. Repeat the process as much as you want. As you move your eyes, they will begin to take in much more visual detail and dilute the stressful thoughts. This added visual information may distract your mind and body from anxiety.

One client, Corrie, had a mild panic attack one day while trying to put her young child down for a nap. This invoked a pattern that caused her to feel uptight and anxious at naptime, a time when she was trying to make her young child relax and be calm in his room. She learned about EMDR and decided to give it a try. As she rocked her child, she moved her eyes from the far left corner of the room to the far right corner of the room. She looked at the different objects—the door knob, the open closet, the clothes hanging up, the picture on the wall, etc. When she got to the far right corner of the room, she would move her eyes back to the left, looking for new objects.

She reported that it worked. After she had several positive experiences using EMDR while putting her child to sleep, the anxiety that regularly came at this time left. EMDR may come in handy during many other types of situations. For example, you may want to try it at a movie, in an airplane, during a meeting, at a dinner party, or in class before a test.

11. Seek Rocking Motion

In many people, rhythmical motion incites a response of the parasympathetic nervous system. We have talked a lot about the sympathetic nervous system that invokes the fight or flight response and accelerates the heart rate, constricts blood vessels, and raises blood pressure. The parasympathetic nervous system, on the other hand, slows the heart rate, increases the intestinal and gland activity, and relaxes the sphincter muscles. These two components of the autonomic nervous system have the exact opposite effect on the body.

When you trigger the parasympathetic nervous system, your body is in a state opposite of the fight or flight response. When infant monkeys were placed in cages with fake surrogate "mothers" that rocked, they displayed significantly more normal behavior than infant monkeys placed in cages with a wire cloth-covered non-rocking surrogate mothers. Researchers concluded the rocking motions helped the monkeys develop brain chemicals necessary for normal behavior.[31]

Some ways to experience a rocking motion are:

- rocking chair
- hammock
- swing
- boating
- horseback riding

12. Cry, Laugh and Smile

Some people will do whatever they can to prevent themselves from crying. What they may not know is that crying can be physically beneficial. When you cry, the body is actually getting rid of a chemical called acetylcholine (known as ACTH) found in tears. The hormone ACTH is a precursor to cortisol, one of the chemicals that promotes the fight or flight response in the body. Allowing yourself a good cry once in a while may actually help regulate brain chemistry.

Likewise, laughter is also healing. Even the word laughter can conjure up past experiences we enjoyed or that uplift our spirits. Not only does laughter have positive effects emotionally, but it also benefits our physical health. One cancer patient watched nothing but videos of Abbott and Costello and other comedies. He felt the progression of his cancer was stopped through the use of laughter.

Smiling, even when forced, is a physical action that is difficult to do and still feel bad inside. Smiling may trigger past experiences that help us relive a joyful time or fun surprise. When we are stressed, take a step outside and smile.

These techniques sound simple. However, their impact should not be minimized. One client suffering from anxiety said that during her most agonizing days she promised herself that every time she passed a certain mirror in her house, she would smile at herself. It took time, but this technique, combined with others, helped her heal and find calmness in her life.

13. Prescribe Your Own Symptoms

When your body becomes anxious, it responds with various physical symptoms or reactions. These symptoms can heighten the anxiety, because it feels like you are physically out of control.

A powerful technique to help relieve anxiety symptoms is to prescribe your own symptoms. This means instead of reacting to the anxiety-related symptoms, you control them by making them worse!

For example, let's say you are going to give a talk in front of a large audience in a few minutes and you are stressed. Your hands are sweaty and shaky. Instead of trying to make the shaking stop (which is a natural response) try and make the symptoms worse. Think about your hands. Think how hot they are. Visualize them shaking uncontrollably. Most likely, these sorts of thoughts will aggravate the symptom for a little while. However, it will also help you feel more control over your body. By prescribing the symptom, the sense of being out of control quickly dissipates because you are now in control of the symptom and have just prescribed the level at which your body reacted. Many times this will make the anxiety-related symptom dramatically lessen and even stop.

Prescribing the symptom changes a sympathetic response to a parasympathetic response, which reduces the adrenalin levels or stops the fight or flight response altogether.

14. Participate in Creative Activities

Involvement in art, music, and creative activities can also reduce stress in our lives. Physiologically speaking, when we engage in creative activities we use our frontal cortex that is typically shut down by the limbic system during times of stress and anxiety. By using our creativity center located in the frontal cortex, we stop the brain from being stuck in a limbic system panic loop. Through drawing, painting, dancing, knitting, writing poetry, and even telling bedtime stories, we access higher order thinking skills and increase serotonin levels in the brain.

Karen came in for treatment because she was often anxious and irritable. While talking, I learned that years before in high school she had enjoyed painting and ballroom dancing. I suggested she utilize these strengths in her life to reduce her stress. She decided to try a weekly dance class and work on her oil paintings. After several weeks, she reported that her anxiousness and high frustration levels were gone. Since she was doing things she loved, she was willing to allocate time for them in her busy schedule. Creative activities add balance and relieve tension and stress.

Developing Resiliency

Some believe a person is either born with resiliency or without it—an attitude of "you've got it or you don't." Scientists have proven, however, that resiliency is a learned trait, not inherited.[32]

How do we develop resiliency? You must face those physical challenges from which you would rather run away and hide. Determination and practice in the end will pay off. As you learn and practice techniques to better manage stress and anxiety, you will find it is through your physical challenges and life's crises that you become resilient.

Weaknesses often become special to us because it is often during physical trials that we find our greatest strength. If we did not have physical trials, we may never learn of what we are capable. One way to encourage resiliency is to learn about how other ordinary people have been resilient.

Some years ago, a young man named Aron Ralston was rock climbing in Utah canyon when an 800-pound boulder shifted above him and his right hand became smashed between the rock and the canyon's sandstone wall.

After spending nearly a week in this position, he ran out of water. Aron resorted to amputating his own hand to free himself from the rock. As he spoke of his ordeal to college students, he told them about returning to the very spot of the accident a few months later. He said, "That place is holy ground for me. . . I don't think I will ever stand on a more powerful spot on all the planet."[33]

He said it was in that very spot—when faced with enormous physical challenges—where he had had the most enlightening experiences of his life. We too will be enlightened about ourselves and what we are capable of when we overcome our physical challenges related to stress and anxiety.

CHAPTER FOUR—Tools to Strengthen Emotional Health

Sariah, Lehi's wife in the *Book of Mormon*, left a beautiful home, a comfortable bed, all her close friends, and her family's riches to follow her husband, the prophet, into the wilderness. She is not a weak woman. However, when she believes her three sons may be dead, her emotions are put to the test and she experiences behavior changes.

In 1 Nephi 5:2, Sariah begins to complain. "She had supposed that we had perished in the wilderness; and she also had complained against my father. . . my sons are no more. . . After this manner of language had my mother complained against my father" (1 Nephi 5:3).

Sariah was emotionally fatigued. Everything that was familiar and safe to her was gone. She feared she had lost her three sons because they haven't returned from their trip to obtain the brass plates from Laban. Lehi tried to comfort her, but it didn't work.

Remember that when someone is having anxiety his or her logic center shuts down. Perhaps that is what happened to Sariah. She knew she should trust Lehi, but emotions had taken over her logical thoughts.

When her sons do return, the scriptures tell us she was comforted. Not only that, but Nephi quotes his mother telling others how her testimony had grown from the experience. She says, "Now I know of a surety that the Lord hath commanded my husband to flee into the wilderness; yea, and I also know of a surety that the Lord hath protected my sons. . . and given them power whereby they could accomplish the thing which the Lord hath commanded them (1 Nephi 5:8).

EMOTIONS AND BEHAVIOR

Early one afternoon a man was driving down the street being tailgated by a stressed-out woman in a mini-van. Suddenly, the traffic light in front of him turns yellow. He chooses the safest choice and stops, even though he could have beaten the red light by accelerating.

The tailgating woman hits her brakes. She yells, screams, swears, waves her arms, and honks the horn incessantly, frustrated she missed her chance to go through the intersection. As she is still in "mid-rant," she hears a tap on her window and looks up into the serious face of a police officer.

The officer orders her to exit the car with her hands up. He takes her to the police station where she is searched, fingerprinted, photographed, and placed in a cell. After a couple of hours, a policeman approaches, opens the cell door, and escorts her back to the booking desk.

"I'm very sorry for this mistake," he says. "You see, I pulled up behind your car while you were blowing your horn, screaming, and swearing at the guy in front of you. I then noticed the 'What Would Jesus Do' window sign, the 'Follow Me to Sunday School' bumper sticker, and the 'I love Jesus' license plate holder. Naturally, I assumed you had stolen the car."

Exaggerated behaviors are often associated with stressful emotions. Often, strong emotions can cause us to be in conflict with who we really are (as seen in the story of the woman in the mini-van). Her emotions caused her to behave in a manner opposite from what she wanted to represent.

What sort of behaviors do you think the woman was engaged in moments before her outburst? Certainly she wasn't sitting in the car with the window down, serenely listening to the birds chirping in the trees. No, she most likely was hunched up, gripping the steering wheel, and glancing at the clock on the dashboard every twenty seconds or so. A behavioral scientist would point out that her actions compounded the anxious emotions she was feeling. When our behavior transforms into actions that are disproportionate to the situation, it is an indicator that we are feeling emotionally out of control.

If we let negative thoughts and behaviors increasingly build, they result in a "lashing out." Fearful emotions are symptoms of stress. Anger often is as well. Difficulty managing negative emotions typically manifests as behavior problems, especially in children. We tend to attack those people we love the very most, such as a spouse, children, parents, friends, or co-workers.

The famous American behaviorist B. F. Skinner believed that most emotions are triggered by behaviors or habits, and if people can learn and unlearn behaviors, they can also learn and unlearn certain emotions. While few psychologist today adhere 100 percent to Skinner's view on emotions, most agree there are definitely strong connections between behavior and emotions. And by changing one, we can often change the other.

Why are We Emotional?

Emotions are tricky to describe at times and even more difficult to study. Everyone's emotions are different because they are subject to interpretation by each individual. Two people can watch the same movie and one person feels exhilarated while the other feels bored. It's the same stimulus with a completely different emotional response.

Some people seem to feel stronger emotions or a wider range of emotions than other people. Researchers have identified four core emotions: fear, anger, sadness and enjoyment. For people with chronic stress and anxiety, the core emotion of fear is more quickly triggered than the other three. Fearful emotions include things such as: dread, worry, panic, abandonment, and vulnerability.

People with anxiety often try to control negative emotions by internalizing them, or keeping them buried within themselves. They are quick to feel fear or panic because the emotion is always there within. Many of my clients with anxiety appear, on the outside, to be put together and in control of their lives. However, under the surface they are struggling.

There are four factors that trigger emotions, particularly those in the fearful genre. They are:

1. Heredity (temperament)
2. Hormonal changes/biological conditions
3. Environmental stimuli
4. Past memories (particularly trauma or abuse as a child)

Emotions are hereditary because they originate in the brain, and the makeup of the brain is genetic. Emotions are created when the limbic system scans for stimuli and sends messages to the to the brain's frontal cortex. The frontal cortex (where our logic and creative centers are located) interprets these messages. This interpretation initiates an emotional response. Hormonal changes also trigger emotions because hormones are catalysts that stimulate various brain activity. If we have hormonal dips or surges, these changes affect the way the brain functions and interprets messages.

When circumstances in our environment start to feel scary or out of control, the amygdala reports it to the frontal cortex. This not only affects current emotions, but we also create memories that associate particular situations with fearful emotions. If we have an experience with a dog that is frightening, most likely future experiences with dogs will also trigger fearful emotions. When someone experiences abuse as a child, various emotional triggers are programmed into their memory. These things may seem unrelated like the color of the carpet where abuse occurred or a certain smell.

EMOTIONAL MANAGEMENT TECHNIQUES:

Changing unwanted emotions is most effective when we incorporate both external (behavioral) and internal (perceptional) techniques. The following tools will help you recognize, shift, change, and manage negative, unwanted emotions.

15. Realize Emotions are not Bad

Some people with stress and anxiety are scared to have any emotions other than happy ones. When we are fearful of emotions (whether consciously or not), we may believe it is wrong to feel sad, bored, nervous, upset, or stress. This is simply not real life. We would never know what enjoyment felt like if we hadn't felt the negative core emotions of fear or anger. No one should expect to be happy all the time. It's not healthy.

When we accept the fact that we all have happy, sad, stressed, and peaceful days, we immediately lower the demands we make emotionally on ourselves. Nobody feels good all the time. Even Christ wept (John 11: 35).

An enlightening exercise is to periodically evaluate our feelings. Using the following list of different emotions, pinpoint emotions you are currently feeling. After evaluating your emotions, ask yourself, "Am I okay with feeling this way?" or "Is this a natural, emotional response to the situation I am in?" If you answer "yes," you know the emotions you are feeling are there for a reason. Learn what the reason is. Don't try to suppress emotions. Ask yourself, "What can I learn from experiencing this feeling?"

If the answers to these questions are "no," the emotions you are feeling may not be constructive. In this situation, you know you may need to change your behavior and thoughts about whatever it is that is triggering these negative emotions.

List of possible emotions you are feeling:

Abandoned	Angry	Anxious
Ashamed	Awkward	Bad
Bitter	Blue	Bored
Calm	Cared about	Closeness
Comfortable	Compassionate	Competent
Content	Daring	Defeated
Defective	Defensive	Discouraged

Down
Embarrassed
Envious
Excited
Foolish
Forgiving
Frightened
Frustrated
Fulfilled
Fun
Furious
Good
Grief
Grudging
Guilty
Happy
Hateful
Hopeful
Hopeless
Humiliated
Imperfect
Inadequate
Incompetent
Inferior
Innocent
Insecure
Interested
Irritated
Joyful
Let down
Lonely
Loved
Mad
Miserable
Moody
Motivated
Neglected
Nervous
On edge
Overly self-aware
Panicky
Paranoid
Peaceful
Pessimistic
Pleased
Productive
Progressive
Proud
Rejected
Relaxed
Remorseful
Resentful
Sad
Scared
Secure
Selfish
Smart
Sorrowful
Stable
Stagnant
Successful
Tense
Terrified
Uncomfortable
Unfulfilled
Unhappy
Unloved
Unproductive
Unstable
Upset
Without pleasure
Worried
Worthless

You may want to use the emotion list on a regular basis for several weeks in order to become more aware of the range of emotions you feel.

When you feel stressed, angry, or depressed, stop and identify your thoughts that occurred right before the emotion surfaced. Ask yourself, "What was I thinking before I became ___________ (type of emotion)?"

As you monitor your thoughts and subsequent feelings, examine how your feelings are connected to your thoughts. For this exercise, ask yourself, "What choices are triggering unwanted feelings?" "How can I change my behavior when I feel this way?"

You will find as you are more aware of your emotions, you will be more willing to feel them and then let go of them instead of hanging onto them or internalizing them. You will also find out which behaviors exacerbate or diminish the emotion. You could even make a list of calming behaviors that work for you.

When you get in a bad mood, use purposeful interventions during the day that create positive feelings. If you try to change your feelings and find you continue to feel overwhelmed, sad, or hopeless, you may be experiencing anxiety-related depression. If it persists, seek professional help through a physician and competent therapist.

16. Avoid Goal Frustration

Unfortunately, self-criticism is a common trait of human nature. We often create self-inflicted guilt or shame that degrades us, eliminates peace from our life, and lowers our ability to improve or reach goals. Eliminating unhealthy guilt is essential in managing emotional stress.

One type of unhealthy guilt comes from unmet goals. As we grow up, we learn in bits and pieces how to set goals, why they are important, and how to achieve them. However, rarely are we taught that unmet goals (a normal part of life) are a source of guilt, stress and even depression.

Take Larry for example. Larry had the goal to have the same kind of family atmosphere in his home as he had growing up. As a child, Larry and his dad worked side by side in the family-owned business. However, as an adult Larry worked at a large corporation. He spent most of his day at the office and many of his nights in front of the computer. It didn't take long for Larry's goal of a close-knit family to catch up with reality. What ensued was a self-inflicted dose of guilt, shame, and anxiety.

When what we want out of life has little to do with how we spend our time each day, stressful emotions result. To help alleviate internal guilt we must match at least some of our daily activities with our major goals in life. When the distance between what we want and what we do grows closer, internal peace returns. The opposite is also true. The further away our behaviors are from our heartfelt goals, the more stress we experience.

Write down four or five of your main goals in life. They don't have to be in any order—just list some important goals at this moment in your life. Some of them may change from year to year, and some of them may stay the same throughout your lifetime.

There are several characteristics of healthy goals. A healthy goal should be one that you have chosen for yourself. Main goals should not conflict with one another. And a healthy goal grows out of a desire to achieve or create something, rather than avoid something.

Once you have written down the goal, write the reason for the goal. Ask yourself, "What is my reason for wanting this goal?" By writing the reason, you see if it qualifies as a major goal and therefore is worth the effort.

Examples:

GOAL: Save $2,000
REASON: To take a special trip with my spouse for our anniversary.

GOAL: Be more patient.
REASON: To be a good example to my children and have joy in parenting.

GOAL:
REASON:

GOAL:
REASON:

GOAL:
REASON:

After you have defined what your main goals are, take several moments throughout the day to write down your daily activities. Break them down into small accomplishments. Now review your daily activities on paper. Did you do something, even for just a few minutes, which helped achieve one or two of your main goals? For example, if one of your goals is to be more patient, did you dedicate a few minutes to meditate? If yes, write that activity below the goal to be more patient. This will remind you that you are involved in the process of achieving that goal. It doesn't matter whether or not you have actually reached it yet.

Maybe you have a goal to grow a flower garden, but you do nothing to regularly achieve that goal. Once you recognize this discrepancy, you can plan a few minutes each day to a small step in that direction. It may be something as simple watering some flower starts in your kitchen window sill.

Our days are filled with so many distractions. Before going to bed, briefly review the things you accomplished that day. This can be on paper, in a journal, or simply in your mind. Be specific! You will see that daily activities are smaller steps to bigger goals. And every small step pushes relieves goal-related guilt and brings emotional peace.

A positive reflection might sound like:

> *What did I get done today? Well, in the morning I exercised for twenty minutes. That felt good and it will probably help me stay calmer during the day (which falls under my goal to be more patient). I also checked out a book from the library about stress (that is under my goal of writing a book.). I hugged my children after bath time (and that was a patient thing to do because they were being wild). I didn't do anything to save money for my trip. Maybe tomorrow I will put back one thing from my shopping cart when I'm at the grocery store and put that money instead in the anniversary trip fund (that will fall under my goal of saving $2,000).*

Reflecting on the positive things you do each day, particularly those things that are in line with main goals, brings internal satisfaction—a sense that you really are moving forward. It really doesn't matter the speed at which you do things, just the direction you are headed. During different times in your life, you may find that you only have one or two main goals because life is so hectic. That's okay. For example, let's say you just had a job change at work and it is very stressful. Your main goals at this time might be 1) to adjust to my new job and 2) spend some time with my family.

One man, Kurt, was experiencing a busy time in his life from a job change, and he decided he needed to get up early to get more time in at work. That meant he had less time with his family. Instead of letting guilt build up inside of him from unmet goals, he planned regular daddy-kid dates on weekends. He no longer felt unmet goal guilt.

17. Relax with Meditation

Using relaxation is a great way to change your emotions. When we relax, we put our bodies in the exact opposite situation as the fight-flight response. Relaxing stimulates the parasympathetic nervous system, and we begin to feel calmer and more peaceful, and we lower our adrenaline and cortisol levels. Reactions of the parasympathetic nervous system include:

- Feelings of calmness, warmth, and relaxation
- Lower blood pressure
- Slower heart rate
- Slower metabolism
- Slower respiration

Relaxing may include things such as meditation, breathing in a pattern, saying prayers, massage, aromatherapy, and many other individual activities. An effective way to relax the mind is to visualize and meditate. In Islamic cultures, a prayer rug is spread out and used to pray at multiple intervals throughout the day. This is done to bring the individual back to a calmer state of being through a connection with God. As Latter-day Saints, we are taught to pray personally both morning and night. Morning prayers are especially effective at setting a relaxed pace throughout the day.

Meditation and Visualization

Our minds are capable of keeping track of thoughts, concerns, ideas and memories upon demand. However, we can become too involved in worries or thoughts that distress us or cause us to become distracted by outside circumstances. Meditation is helpful in bringing about a heightened state of personal consciousness, relaxation, or enlightenment, and reversing the overload we place on our minds. Visualization involves bringing about a change in the physical being by using the power of the mind.

Meditation and visualization are not always easy to do, especially when just beginning. In fact, they use one of the parts of our body we often forget to work out—the brain. However, both meditation and visualization are excellent tools for people with stress and anxiety because the same imagination that fuels the mind with fears and worries also has the power to be creative in a calming manner.

In the book, *Way to Be*, President Gordon B. Hinckley talks about his father who would go sit on a rock wall for hours. On that wall he would think. President Hinckley encourages all to find their own rock wall, to spend some time in nature, and to get to know themselves.[34] In the *Book of Mormon*, after a particularly stressful time preaching the gospel, Alma takes his companion Amulek to his house and helps him relax and gain strength spiritually (Alma chapter 15).

There are a lot of different ways to meditate. An example of meditation is when you're driving a car and thinking of something so intensely that it takes away your awareness of where you are or what you are doing. Suddenly you come to and remember you are in the car. This is a type of meditation. In meditation, you eliminate the chatter of the mind—the constant thinking, planning, and worrying. As you reduce the negative arousal of the mind, stress and anxiety are also reduced. To meditate, some people choose a mantra (a word or simple sound) and repeat it over and over while in a comfortable position. Some choose a coping or inspirational statement such as a line from an inspirational poem. Other people focus on their abdominal breathing pattern. Another way is to visualize a peaceful scene in your mind. This is called visual imagery.

Whichever way you choose to meditate, here are a few basic guidelines:

1. Find a quiet place where you can be alone if possible.
2. Sit or lay in a comfortable position.
3. Loosen your clothing so you can breathe using abdominal breaths.
4. Uncross your legs or arms.
5. Close your eyes and take several abdominal breaths.
6. Start to visualize a particular object or scene in nature.
7. When your mind drifts from the scene, don't get upset. Let distracting thoughts come into your mind, let them pass through, and then continue with the meditation.

8. When meditating on a scene in nature, try to use all of your five senses. Think about the beauty you would **see**, the sounds you **hear**, **smells** that are pleasant, **tastes** that are delicious, and **feelings** that are comforting or relaxing. By involved the five senses, your meditation will feel more real and it will help relax the entire body and intensify your meditation.

The following is an example of a visualization exercise. Focus your thoughts on the following scenario.

> *You are walking down a rock path. You hear the crunch of the pebbles under your feet. You see the red and gray colors in the rock. As you slowly walk forward, you notice green bushes growing on either side of the rock path. These bushes grow taller the further down the rock path you walk. As you walk, you feel a gentle breeze on your cheek. You use nice, steady steps to approach a large wooden door. The handle on the door has a key hole, and you happen to have a key around your neck that fits exactly. As you unlock the door, you hear a click and feel the weight of the door as you open it. You are happy to see inside the door a secret garden, filled with flowers, meadows, waterfalls, trees, birds, etc. . . You walk into the secret garden and shut the door behind you. This is your place. You have all the time you need here.*

In the secret garden, take time to look at all the beauty in nature around you. Maybe you imagine a baby deer getting a drink in a pool of water. Maybe you hear birds, taste the spray from the waterfall, touch the grass with your feet, lean on a tree, or smell the flowers. Spend about ten minutes in your garden.

In addition to meditation, there are other ways to relax. We've already mentioned a few of these—massage therapy; listening to peaceful, repetitive music; muscle relaxation, aromatherapy, yoga to name a few. Remember, relaxation is a learned activity. It takes practice, especially if you aren't in the habit of doing it very often.

Sometimes you may want to use relaxation, but you feel too wound up to make it effective. In this situation, perform a muscle tension/relaxation exercise first (See Chapter Three). Practice the muscle tension/relaxation exercise several times until you have depleted the adrenaline in your body. Now you will be ready to effectively do a visual imagery exercise or a different relaxing activity.

18. Incorporate Self-Rejuvenating Activities into Life

People with chronic stress and anxiety are often the same people who rarely give themselves a break. They rarely do things for themselves. They may be embarrassed and insistent that they don't need anything. Research has shown, however, that by doing activities that nurture or rejuvenate one's self a person becomes more emotionally and physically healthy. We need to care for things that are valuable to us, including ourselves.

Time management expert Stephen Covey tells of a man in the woods sawing down a tree. He is exhausted from working for hours. Someone suggests he take a break to sharpen his saw, but he replies, "I can't. I don't have time to sharpen the saw. I'm too busy sawing!"[35]

This is often how stressed people approach life. They are too busy living and being stressed to improve their lives. Finding time to nurture oneself through rejuvenating activities relieves us of the stress of doing only things we have to and nothing we want to.

At the end of this section is a list of suggested self-rejuvenating activities. If none of these sound good to you, don't worry. You can make your own list. One of the best ways to discover activities that speak to you is to reflect back upon what you enjoyed doing as a child, before adulthood hit. What did you do for fun when you were eight, or twelve, or sixteen?

One couple reflected together on what they did as children that brought them enjoyment. The husband remembered going on long bike rides. The wife remembered crocheting and doing handiwork with her mother. Neither of them had done either of these activities in years. So, he bought a bike and she got back into handiwork. Now, when one of them starts getting grumpy or stressed, the other reminds him or her to go biking or do some handiwork.

Self-rejuvenating activities replenish the soul, calm our emotions, and remind us that life is too important to neglect the things we really love to do.

60 Self-Rejuvenating Activities

1. Listen to your favorite music
2. Enjoy a long, warm bubble bath
3. Go for a walk and listen to the sounds of nature on the way
4. Share a hug with a loved one
5. Exercise—even if it is just for ten minutes
6. Spiritual prayer during which you thank God for your blessings
7. Do stretching exercises—animals do this for a good reason
8. Reflect on positive qualities. "I am…" List 20 of yours

9. Watch the sunrise or sunset
10. Laugh about something you remember from your past
11. Meditate on a relaxing scene
12. Get a massage
13. Reflect on: "I appreciate…"
14. Write thoughts and feelings in a personal journal
15. Attend a favorite athletic event
16. Do something adventurous
17. Read a book or magazine
18. Sing/hum/whistle a tune from your childhood
19. Swing/slide/teeter totter
20. Play a musical instrument
21. Work with plants (gardening)
22. Learn a new skill through a neighbor or a class
23. Go to a play or movie
24. Ride a bike/motorcycle
25. Make a gourmet meal/dessert
26. Draw/paint a picture
27. Swim/float/wade/relax in a pool
28. Do aerobics or dance
29. Visit a place from your childhood
30. Smile to yourself in the mirror and say, "I love myself."
31. Go horseback riding
32. Reflect on: "My most enjoyable memories are…"
33. Visit a museum or art gallery
34. Practice yoga or pilates
35. Relax in a whirlpool/sauna
36. Count your blessing: "I am thankful for…"

37. Star gaze
38. Window shop
39. Go to the library
40. Daydream on purpose
41. Go sailing or paddle boating
42. Reward myself with a special gift I can afford (i.e. a music CD)
43. Take a day trip or vacation
44. Create something with clay/pottery
45. Pet an animal
46. Reflect on successes: "I can…"
47. Sew something simple
48. Attend a symphony
49. Write a poem
50. Make a bouquet of flowers
51. Watch the clouds and find shapes in them
52. Visit a park/woods/forest
53. Read positive, motivational literature
54. Reflect on: "What I value most in life…"
55. Phone an old friend
56. Go on a picnic
57. Enjoy a cup of herbal tea or hot chocolate
58. Participate in your favorite sport/game/recreational activity
59. Listen to a relaxation tape
60. Create your own unique list of self-rejuvenating activities

19. Journal

Journaling is an excellent tool to change negative emotions. The process of writing may help manage stress and anxiety by:

- reducing obsessive thoughts that are bothersome
- identifying emotional triggers
- expressing internalized feelings
- focusing thoughts
- increasing honesty with yourself
- helping you plan for the future
- promoting gratitude for the good in life
- being a record of past accomplishments
- reminding you of supportive people who love you
- tracking progress

When you journal, the most important thing to do is be completely honest in what you write. This may mean you keep a journal to pass on to your children and keep another journal just for you. In the personal journal, express your fears and stresses freely. After all, what you write is truly just for you.

The physical action of writing out thoughts and feelings helps bring things into perspective. Some people choose to journal only when things feel tense. Others choose to journal on a regular basis.

Wendy had kept a journal since she was a teenager. She was now the mom of a handful of boys, and she knew she didn't feel quite right. Her emotions had seemed to be off for some time, but she kept telling herself she was fine. Her husband told her several times, "I think you need help. You don't seem yourself," but she assumed he was being overly protective. Then one day she decided to read back in her journal.

She was shocked to see how negative her entries for the past several months had been. She had always shared her feelings freely in her journal, and it was these journal entries that helped her recognize she was going through something more difficult than she wanted to admit. The journal entry that pushed her to seek professional assistance had only one word: HELP. It was written across the upper half of the page in large letters, and she only vaguely remembered writing it.

She knew her journal didn't lie, and so she got help. She saw her doctor who sent her to an internist. A physical ailment that compounded anxiety and depression was diagnosed, and she received professional help. Her journal made her listen when nobody else could.

She says one of the most rewarding things for her to do now is to read back in her journal and see how much progress she has made. Her journal has become her lifeline to reality. She has learned to trust herself to write down the things her emotions are really trying to tell her.

20. Desensitize Yourself

Desensitization is when you slowly expose or reintroduce yourself to an event, place, or situation that gave you stress or anxiety in the past. Often, our minds are reminded of an emotionally frightening experience through a related object or place. Even after the stress is gone, when we see particular objects or places, our bodies have an intense emotional reaction.

For example, one woman accompanied her sick child on an emergency helicopter life flight to a distant hospital. Several months after the incidence, she saw a billboard on the freeway that showed a picture of a helicopter. She was surprised when her body began to panic with her heart pounding, shallow breathing, and sweating. She emotionally started to feel out of control. Desensitization can help us rid ourselves of uncomfortable emotions associated with certain objects or places (or even people).

Let's say you were sitting in a particular chair when you received a distressing phone call. Ever since the phone call, you may feel some anxiety sitting in that chair. You may need to desensitize yourself to the chair. You could do this several ways. One way would be by creating new, positive associations with the chair. You may try to sit in that chair to do some relaxation exercise or breathing techniques. Or maybe you could make the chair a place of honor at the next family meal. Everybody in the family says something nice to the person in the chair. These positive associations will help you change the feelings you have about something by easing back into it while using relaxing techniques to lower your anxiety.

Another way to desensitize yourself is to expose yourself slowly but regularly to an anxiety provoking situation or object. By avoiding a place or situation that gives you stress, you reconfirm in your mind that the place or situation really is scary. If you face your fear, you will be able to overcome it. I know a man who was physically fit but he didn't like to take his shirt off when swimming because of rude comments he had overheard about himself when he was a boy. For him, working up to the point where he could take his shirt off for the entire time he was at a swimming pool helped him get over some of his unfounded insecurities he had about his appearance.

If it is not feasible to physically desensitize yourself to your fear, you can do it in your mind's eye. For example, I know a woman who had anxiety over the fear of contracting a horrible disease. She realized it was an unfounded fear, and so she decided to desensitize herself to it. She couldn't really give herself the disease, but she could visualize herself getting the disease. She took ten minutes each day for several weeks and visualized herself with this disease. At first, the desensitization increased her stress. However, each time she visualized herself with the disease, she asked herself, "Could I handle this?" As she saw herself in the fearful situation over and over, she slowly desensitized herself to the fear of the disease. After a little more than a week she got to the point in her visualizations where she answered, "Yes, I could handle this."

If you try this sort of desensitization, try relaxing breathing to bring your stress level down while you gently expose yourself to the stressful situation or object. Afterward, you can also try peaceful meditation to once again bring your stress down.

These sorts of techniques are called exposure and cognitive flooding, and they are often used in anxiety or phobia treatment. These exercises help subdue and overcome the fear response prevalent in people with stress and anxiety. If the fears are extremely disturbing, a mental health professional should help with this process.

21. Change the Routine

If you have chronic stress in your life, you may need to change your routine to change your emotions. We all get into routines—sometimes they are healthy, sometimes they are not. Take Don for instance. Don was an engineer with an exciting but demanding job. He loved what he did. However, after several years at his job, he noticed he was becoming anxious and stressed on the way home from work. He talked it over with a trusted friend. She asked him, "What is the last thing you do before leaving work each evening?"

He thought about it and answered, "I check my email. There are usually several things brought up in my email that I need to get to, but I can't because I'm about to leave for home." Immediately a light went on in Don's mind. He realized that he should avoid checking his e-mail right before leaving for home. It was creating stress in his life that was impossible for him to reduce while driving home. While this may seem obvious, we are often so tied to our routines that we don't realize how damaging they may be.

Another woman, Janice, was a mother of three young children. Her husband was very busy with his law practice and a member of an LDS bishopric. Janice, a calm, collected, and talented woman, was shocked when she began having mild panic attacks during church meetings. What was going on?

She talked it over with a friend who asked her what her Sunday mornings were like. Janice answered, "Awful! My husband is always gone and I am overwhelmed with trying to get the children looking nice. I always run out of time to get myself ready. Once we're at church, I feel self conscious at being only half put together. When my children act up, I feel like everyone is looking at me, and that is the last thing I want."

After talking the problem over, Janice decided to change her Sunday morning routine. Instead of getting her children ready first, she got herself ready. She made sure she felt presentable, and then she helped the children get ready. She made several other changes as well, and by changing her routine the panic attacks stopped.

To change an unhealthy routine, you first need to identify exactly when you felt negative emotions from stress. For Don it was driving home from work. For Janice it was in church. Next, think about the things you did leading up to the stress. What was I involved with before the stress occurred? Is there a routine I am following that I don't even realize? How can I change my routine?

Along with changing your routine, you may want to add something to it. At times of high anxiety, stress, or depression, it may be a chore just getting out of bed in the morning. People experiencing chronic stress may wake up with a lump in their stomach just thinking about starting a new day. In a situation like this, it may be beneficial to add something you love to do to your routine first thing in the morning.

Perhaps you could garden for twenty minutes as soon as the children are off to school. Another idea may be staying in the car in the parking lot before work and give yourself fifteen minutes to read one chapter of a good book. Whatever the scenario, by finding time to do one activity you enjoy you enhance your routine and increase the number of positive emotions that are connected to the start of each day.

22. Connect with Your "Child-like Self"

Most adults assume their childhood is long past, but the truth of the matter is most of us still have child-like needs. We tend to ignore these needs, however, and be critical of them. These child-like elements are emotional dimensions of us that feel alive, young, energetic, excited, and creative. There is also no doubt that our child-like self is more connected to our emotions and fears than our adult self. Reconnecting with this part of you may help you be more aware of your emotions and better understand the reasons for feeling the way you do.

So how do you emotionally reconnect with your child-like self? There are various ways.

A simple way to reconnect with your child-like self is to play like a child. Do something you loved to do as a kid. Go to a playground and actually play. Play games with your own children—roll on the grass, splash in mud puddles, or jump in a pile of leaves. Color a picture in a coloring book, try finger painting or paint your face like a clown.

Sparking childhood memories is also effective in reconnecting with your younger self. You may want to begin by getting a photo of yourself when you were a child. Try to bring up a dialogue with yourself as a child. You may choose to do this through letter writing. Write a letter to yourself as if talking to yourself as a child. Ask questions like, “How do you feel?” and “What do you love and fear the most?” Once that is completed, write a letter that is your child’s response. Don’t plan what you will write. Just sit down and start writing. This is called free flow writing.

Instead of writing a letter, you may want to take ten minutes to visualize a conversation with your child-like self. Actually picture yourself speaking to you as a child. This sort of exercise may need to be repeated for several days or weeks before an insightful conversation takes place. This may be especially helpful to those who experienced trauma as a child.

The following is personal experience one of my clients shared with me after she worked on reconnecting with her child-like self:

> *The first time I invited my child-like self to talk to me was an insightful experience. It helped me realize that for decades I had been trying to understand why no one stopped abuse I endured as a child. Even as an adult, my child-like self still sought to know why I had been disappointed by the adults in my life. I told myself that I was now an adult, and I would be the protector of the hurt child inside of me.*
>
> *This knowledge was powerful. I now recognize that when my child-like self feels fearful, I need to listen. The emotions are real, and as an adult I can face them and not run away.*

23. Create Personal Relationships

Relationships are important. They often create our most stressful and intense feelings as well as our most pleasant and happy emotional experiences.

Research has shown that bonding with an average of twelve support people helps reduce stress. Friends or family members can listen to our feelings, show love and support, and give us feelings of comfort and security from which we can gain strength. We, in return, can do the same for them.

Nurturing activities with friends or family members can include appropriate physical touch such as back rubs, foot rubs, hugs, etc... Social activities help us forget ourselves and enjoy others through laughter, meaningful communication, and sharing similar experiences.

Take a moment and think about the people in your life. Make a list of those whom you would consider your "support group." Do you give as well as receive from these people? Do you have very many people you can turn to? Is there someone close by with whom you could create a healthy relationship?

Isabelle was going through a return bout of anxiety. She had moved since her first experience with anxiety, and she realized most of her support group lived far away. She decided to strike up some new friendships. She called a neighbor woman she had often seen out running and asked if she could join her twice a week on her run. The neighbor agreed. Isabelle learned her neighbor had also experienced some anxiety and depression, and the two of them connected on several different levels. The relationship helped Isabelle at a particularly hard time.

To create supportive friends, you may need to be the one who first makes an effort. If you do this, friendships will follow. You don't want to be overbearing and expectant of others. Any supportive relationship should be a win-win experience. Within your relationships, it is helpful to learn how to talk about feelings. There are some basic skills we can all work on to effectively communicate feelings. Here is a quick list of do and don'ts.

Do:

- Create a safe/positive environment
- Use "I" statements
- Invite and then listen to the other person's feelings and thoughts
- Focus on the solution, not the problem

Don't:

- Bring up the past
- Give excuses
- Be defensive
- Use "you" statements
- Get angry

24. Prepare for Time Outs

People who feel chronic stress in their lives can make a basket or duffle bag of their favorite things. In times of high stress, go to the basket or duffle bag and take a time out. This will help restore control in your life. If we take the time before we are stressed to plan things we like to do, then when we are stressed (and our logic and creative brains centers aren't working as well), we can still come up with creative activities because of our planning.

When you participate in an activity that you particularly enjoy, the experience can create an emotional feeling of control in your life that is missing during stress or anxiety. Doing activities you enjoy may:

- help you feel in more control of your emotions
- give you an altered sense of time
- increase the clarity of other situations
- integrate mind and body
- slow down a hectic-paced life
- comfort you when you are overwhelmed

In your time out bag, you may want to include things like your favorite CD, a good book, a soft blanket, a game, smells you love like a candle or perfume, phone numbers of supportive friends or family, a craft, some of your hobbies, a special treat, a back "scratcher," a favorite picture, etc…

I know after a hectic day of work, I come home and feel tired, but I'm not quite ready for bed. In my time out basket I keep things that I can do to help me lower stress levels and unwind. One of my favorites is a computer CD that takes me on a tour of all of the exotic places in the world that I would love to visit. After indulging in this creative, stress reducing activity, my body is both physically and emotionally ready for sleep.

25. Allow Yourself to Grieve

One of the most difficult emotional tests to endure is dealing with the loss of a loved one. Much has been written about the stages of grief. First there is disbelief that the death has really occurred, a numbness or denial of the loss, depression and anger. Eventually there is a resuming of daily activities, and then finally a time of reinvesting in building a life without the loved one.

When tragic things happen, many of us don't allow ourselves to grieve. However, each of these stages is vital to emotionally getting back on our feet. So many people skip the steps of grief and in so doing cause the grief to simmer within them, cankering their emotional well-being. Once we have moved through the steps of grief, life can and will continue.

Michelle was having a difficult time grieving and consequently was experiencing a lot of anxiety. She felt that if she didn't constantly think about her brother, who had died recently, it would mean she didn't love him. She felt guilty for feeling happy or excited about anything because that meant she wasn't "remembering" him and his tragic death. Hearing this dream from someone else finally helped her to let go. This was the dream:

> *I was doing the housework and chores to care for my family. I noticed that chained to my leg was my husband who had passed away. Everywhere I went I had to pull him along with me. As I went up the stairs to clean, I had to carry my husband upstairs too. As I went on errands, I had to load my husband into the car and take him along. As I vacuumed, dusted, and swept, I was never alone. In the dream I remember being exhausted. I realized that carrying the grief and pain with me of my husband's loss was only hurting me and wearing me out.*

When the woman awoke, she knew she had to let herself go through the grieving process. In so doing, she could symbolically detach herself from the guilt she had been feeling about trying to enjoy life again. Eventually she was able to move forward.

Grief takes tremendous energy, yet it never changes the fact that we have experienced a loss. While we must go through the grieving process, the challenge is to eventually re-engage in life and use our energy and time in ways that help us grow, serve others, and develop talents. Fixations, obsessions, and fears are signs of an emotionally hurting person.

Refining Yourself

My grandmother lived in San Francisco in the early 1900s. She often lamented that most of her family's belongings were destroyed during the great San Francisco fire. One keepsake, however, did make it through the fire—a small ceramic vase. In the heat of the fire, steel melted, furniture turned to ashes, and walls crumbled, but the vase survived. In fact, the vase is more beautiful than before. The fire could not damage the vase because it had already been through intense heat when it was made. In the end, the ravaging fire actually brought out more color in the vase and created bubbles in its porcelain to create a unique and vibrant masterpiece.

At times we are placed in situations in life where we are put through a refining fire. We must trust that despite the hard times, we are meant for success. An anonymously authored story talks of a group of women that met for Bible study each week. While studying, they came across a phrase that talked about being refined in a refiner's fire (Malachi 3:3).

One of the women offered to find out more about the process of refining silver and get back to the group at their next meeting. She called up a silversmith and he agreed to let her watch him while he worked. She observed him holding a piece of silver over the fire and letting it heat up. He explained when refining silver, one had to hold the silver in the middle of the fire, where the flames were the hottest, in order to burn away the impurities. He also explained that he had to keep his eyes on the silver the entire time the silver was being heated. If not, it could ruin.

The woman was silent for a moment. Then she asked, "But how do you know when the silver is fully refined?" He answered, "Oh, that's easy—it's ready when I can see my reflection in it."

President Harold B. Lee, a kind and compassionate LDS prophet, experienced emotional trials described in the book, *Harold B. Lee: Prophet and Seer*. The author, Brent Goates, uses the prophet's journal and other sources to recount a period of time in President Lee's life that was filled with anxiety and emotional turmoil.[36]

After being an apostle for more than twenty years, President Lee's wife Fern died from a terminal illness. At the time, President Lee was an apostle. He had been a caregiver to his wife during her illness. After Fern passed away on September 24, 1962, President Lee gathered his family together and beautifully taught them of love, life, and death. Regardless of his knowledge of the plan of salvation, inside he was emotionally aching, exhausted, and suffering. The next month he gave two talks in General Conference and reported in his journal that he was "totally exhausted."

Instead of getting better, his emotional shut down continued. His journal records sleepless nights. In November of that year he fulfilled a Church-related assignment to Europe where President Lee wrote in his journal, "Nervous tensions and depression turned last night into a nightmare." Because of his nervousness, President Lee stayed away from meetings and stayed to himself. His traveling companion wrote, "I have seen him weep on many occasions."

During the next few months his emotional battle continued. He remarked during this time that it was difficult to have the spirit with him during his sermons. Little by little, however, President Lee's emotions began to heal, only to be placed in the Refiner's fire once more.

In 1965, President Lee, still an apostle, received a call that his daughter was having difficulties delivering her fifth child. A few minutes later President Lee received the news she had died. His daughter's death seemed to unveil the same emotions he had felt at his wife's death. He again began to suffer from sleeplessness, feelings of being overwhelmed, and nervousness. He wrote, "I could hardly control myself physically or emotionally."

Eventually health returned and President Lee's trials "filled his heart with empathy for all other sufferers." He served as an apostle for thirty-one years, and was prophet for seventeen months.

During his church service, President Lee became one of the major driving forces behind the LDS Church's highly successful Welfare Program. He was continually concerned for the physical, emotional, and spiritual needs of others. In his memoriam, it was written of him, "He warmed the hearts of the many he touched with a special glow. He moved with the swiftness of energy, but a child could catch up with him and, unafraid, take his hand. He was direct and vigorous, but nothing could be gentler than his arm, circling an aged sister's shoulders while he bent to listen to her words."[37]

He had been through the Refiner's fire and had come out more brilliant and exquisite than ever. The same can be true for all of us.

CHAPTER FIVE—Tools to Strengthen Mental Health

In the *Old Testament,* when the Lord tells Jonah he needs to go to Nineveh and preach the gospel, Jonah's thoughts begin to focus on the negative. First he tells himself the people of the Nineveh don't deserve the gospel. Next he convinces himself he doesn't want to go to Nineveh because he is sure he will be killed. And then, in a rather illogical way, he decides he will run away from God. His thoughts create a fearful situation.[38]

As Jonah tries to hide from God on a ship, a storm comes and Jonah's shipmates confront him. He confesses, "I fear the Lord, the God in Heaven" (Jonah 1:9). His shipmates toss him off the boat and Jonah finds himself in the belly of a big fish.

Inside the fish, Jonah wrestles with his thoughts. While most of us think that being swallowed by a fish would be more frightening than preaching the gospel, the experience does not immediately change Jonah's negative thinking. Instead, he must weigh in his mind his present situation with that of going to Nineveh.

In the end, and with the help of the Holy Ghost, Jonah exclaims in chapter 2 verse 9, "I will sacrifice unto thee with the voice of thanksgiving; I will pay that that I have vowed. Salvation is of the Lord." He faces his fears, changes his thoughts, adjusts his behavior, and travels to Nineveh.

We Act How We Think

When Judy started therapy she felt panicked, ashamed, and desperate. She knew what was bothering her—it was unwanted thoughts. Thoughts of hurting herself or those she loved would pop into her head at unexpected times. These thoughts made her feel as if she was a bad person and they were occurring more frequently. She constantly questioned whether she was a good mother or wife. Fearing that because she had what she called "evil" thoughts, she must be evil herself.

Judy had obsessive-compulsive disorder (an anxiety-related disorders discussed in Chapter Two). Her obsessive thoughts of hurting herself or others made her feel unclean. In an effort to feel clean, she would wash her hands dozens of times throughout the day or clean her house excessively (to the point of cleaning all the window corners and cracks with a toothbrush each day). She didn't realize it, but she performed these outward compulsions to gain a sense of control over her fears and anxieties.

Not everyone with unwanted thoughts has OCD. In fact, we all experience times when we would like to change our thinking. Some people with anxiety may have repetitive thoughts without compulsions. Whatever the situation, thoughts can be anxiety evoking.

Using a combination of medication and therapy, Judy found stillness. She learned techniques to change her thinking patterns, and her life improved. Judy had to learn that thoughts create feelings, and feelings create behaviors. In the last chapter we focused on how to better manage negative feelings or unwanted emotions. In this chapter, we are going to discuss how to change our thinking, which will result in changed behavior.

Hardwiring

Worrisome, anxious thoughts create stress and anxiety. Thoughts, and our reactions to those thoughts, are not random. Thinking is a process that is largely a learned behavior. While we may be born more of a pessimist or more of an optimist in temperament, with experience we override some of our natural tendencies and change thought processes.

The typical brain cell, or neuron, is made up of many parts, particularly the axon and dendrites. Think of it like a tree where the axon is the trunk of a tree, the axon terminals are the tree roots (message senders) and the dendrites (or message receivers) are the tree branches.

The brain creates pathways for our thoughts to travel upon by hardwiring neurons together. This is done by ordering neurons in a line (end to end) with a small space in between the dendrites of one cell and the axon terminals of the other cell. The empty space in between the two is called the synapse. Brain messages travel through the synapse using brain chemicals (called neurotransmitters). Some of the most common brain neurotransmitters included serotonin, dopamine, norepinephrine, and epinephrine. As the brain sends repeated messages down a string of neurons, they become hardwired, meaning the synapses between the neurons becomes more easily traveled.

There are two ways the brain hardwires neurons. The first method is through a learned response. A learned response is a habit like tying your shoes, driving a car, or brushing your teeth. These are things we don't think about doing anymore because from hardwiring the brain knows exactly how to do them. It takes several weeks or months of repetitive action to hardwire neurons together in a learned response.

The second way the brain hardwires neurons together is through a traumatic/emotional experience. This type of hardwiring happens at the moment a person experiences a traumatic or highly emotionally charged situation. Instead of being a learned response, this type of hardwiring is created by the brain through the presence of an enormous amount of epinephrine. The brain will return to this hardwired neuron pathway each time the same or similar circumstances present themselves.

Traumatic hardwiring is the reason that objects or places can invoke unsolicited fear and panic. Becky had been feeling worried about something all day so she decided to exercise. She put on some energetic music and began running on the treadmill. During her workout, while thinking about her worries she experienced a mild panic reaction. A few weeks later, Becky was on the treadmill again. This time she was not worried at all but was into her workout when the same song she had been listening to weeks before began to play. Her body immediately started a panic reaction like the one from weeks ago even though she been feeling fine and was not stressed. Her earlier panic had created a hardwired response to the situation of being on the treadmill listening to that particular song.

After learning about hardwiring, Becky decided to create a new pathway for her neurons. She did this by getting on the treadmill and purposely listening to the song that invoked a negative hardwired response. However, during the song she thought of relaxing things, and she rewarded herself when it was over. It didn't take her long to recreate more positive hardwired pathways associated with the treadmill.

Creating New Pathways

Like Becky, we can all change our hardwired pathways and create more healthy thinking patterns. When babies are born, their brains contain billions of random neurons. As babies grow and learn new things, repeated behaviors hardwire neurons together. In this way children learn to talk, walk, and even read. They also learn to think in a certain way.

We can change both negative learned hardwiring and traumatic or emotional hardwiring through positive learned hardwiring. Recognize that depending on the length of time neurons have been hardwired, it can take an average person two months to two years to create an alternative (better) pathway for neurons to travel down. While changing hardwired neuron pathways takes practice and time, it is well worth the effort.

Diana had anxiety each time she got near a swimming pool because she had a near-drowning experience as a child. This was a traumatic hardwired response. By using a combination of physical, emotional and mental techniques, she created a new learned response to water. The new response was one that didn't involve anxiety.

Robert told himself he was fat each time he looked in the mirror. This habit caused him stress and destroyed his confidence. He had to work on repetitively telling himself affirming thoughts each time he approached a mirror. After a period of constant reaffirmation, he changed his hard wired negative response when looking into a mirror.

We feel how we think. If we are in a negative, unhealthy pattern of thinking, then most likely we feel negative and uncomfortable. If we are in a healthy, positive pattern of thinking, we feel positive and healthy. This doesn't mean that stress won't come to those who have positive thinking patterns. It does mean, however, that when the stressful situations come, a person who uses healthy thinking patterns will react and respond in a healthier, more effective way.

MENTAL MANAGEMENT TECHNIQUES:

26. Try Positive Affirmation

After serving in the U.S. military as a pilot during World War II, Og Mandino landed a job as a magazine editor. Years later, in 1968, he published a book called *The Greatest Salesman in the World.* The book takes the form of a parable that encourages the reader to repeat positive, statements to him or herself each day over a period of time. What Og Mandino did was incorporate the psychological principle of positive affirmation into his writing. It worked, and he sold more than thirty million copies of his book.

Positive affirmation is a powerful tool, but it's one that takes time, commitment, and honesty. You can do your own positive affirmation exercise by writing down twenty-five things that are good about yourself. These should begin "I am. . . " and you fill in the blank with an honest, complementary statement about yourself. This may be hard to do for some people who are in negative thinking patterns, so take a look at some of the following examples:

Examples of Positive Affirmations

- I am teachable
- I am genuinely kind
- I am a talented singer
- I am a good organizer
- I am funny

- I am strong
- I am physically fit
- I am determined
- I am loving
- I am easy to love
- I am a good listener
- I am a good friend
- I am successful at work
- I am an effective manager
- I am a clean person
- I am spontaneous

Each morning for at least two months, take a few minutes and read your positive affirmations. Read them again at night. As you read them, believe them. This repetition creates a new neuron pathway for your thoughts. The more you repeat them, the more these positive statements will become the natural way you think about yourself.

Continue with this exercise as long as needed. You may want to keep your positive affirmations and pull them out from time to time and make sure you still believe each positive statement about yourself. To work, a positive affirmation must be positive. It must begin with "I am" and be honest.

27. Identify Unhealthy Thinking Patterns

For years, Mary thought about her life the same way—trials were bad and she must avoid them at all cost. Despite how hard she tried, life brought her challenges nonetheless. When this happened, Mary experienced serious anxiety.

She sought help and realized she had a number of distorted ways of thinking about life. Learning about and recognizing unhealthy thinking patterns greatly helped Mary view life and its difficulties more calmly.

Just like Mary, many of us don't realize we harbor unhealthy thinking patterns. The following are examples of common unhealthy thinking patterns that can be reversed with the right tools, work, and patience.

- believing that worrying solves problems
- blowing things out of proportion
- categorical or "black and white" thinking
- comparison thinking
- dwelling on the negative
- fear of rejection/need for approval
- perfectionism
- "what if" thinking
- "should" thinking

<u>Worrying solves problems</u>—For one reason or another, many of us erroneously believe that if we worry enough we can solve problems or prevent bad things from happening. Worrying does little, however, except raise our stress and anxiety levels.

By trying to control our outside circumstances with worry, we typically create unhealthy conditions inside the body. Instead of worrying, look for creative solutions to solve problems. Step out of the worry box and be constructive. Tell yourself, "If I am worrying about something I can't control, I need to let go and focus on something else."

<u>Blowing things out of proportion</u>—In many computer programs, there is a tool called the "zoom" tool. By clicking on the icon of the magnifying glass you can "zoom in" to see minute details in a picture or document. Many of us mentally "zoom in" to life's circumstances and blow their importance or gravity out of proportion. When we magnify the importance of things to be larger or more serious than they really are, we set ourselves up to feel more stress. Taking a step back and "zooming out" allows us to see the larger picture and realize the situation isn't as enormous as first assumed. Ask yourself, "Will this matter in two weeks or even in a year from now?" If the answer is no, let it go.

<u>Categorical thinking</u>—Categorical thinking is when we think in absolutes: black and white, good and bad, success or failure. Normally, a child thinks categorically until around the age of eight. When a child is about eight, he or she is mature enough to start thinking logically. As a child near puberty, he or she begins abstract thinking, which allows a person to view things in shades of gray. When little children make mistakes, they assume they are bad. Or when children see someone doing something naughty, they assume the person is bad. This is because young children only have the ability to think in black or white (concrete) concepts.

When our brain matures, we have the ability to think abstractly and process situations using different perspectives. However, when we are anxious or angry, we often go back to categorical thinking. As an adult, categorical thinking is unhealthy because rarely is something or someone all good or a total success. If you insist on putting characteristics, accomplishments, and other such things into tidy categories, nothing ever measures up. The opposite of categorical thinking is process thinking.

The joy and satisfaction comes in the process, or in other words, in the learning. Thinking things such as, "Sure, the book I wrote isn't perfect, but I learned a lot doing it," is a thought that focuses more on the process than on the absolute. One mistake doesn't wipe out all the good. If we learn from mistakes and move on in the right direction, we will grow and reduce our stress.

Comparison thinking—When we compare ourselves to others or to unrealistic expectations, we invite stress and anxiety into our lives. Comparison thinking is flawed because we are comparing ourselves (about whom we know the bad and the good) to people about whom we typically only know the good. Comparison thinking is an easy trap to fall into, and it is behind much of the stress and anxiety some people feel. For example, "He works out longer than I do in the gym, so I am not as good as he is" or "Her children have such cute clothes on. She must be a better mother than I am." The examples of comparison thinking are endless, and they are almost always destructive.

Dwelling on the negative—When we dwell on the negative, it is like we are taking a filter and literally straining out everything positive from our lives. It is more than just seeing the glass half full or half empty. It is obsessing on the empty. We all see things differently, but when we dwell on only the negative, or when we change everything into a negative, we cause ourselves sadness and misery. Filtering out the positive is a learned behavior that elicits heightened stress and anxiety in almost any situation. However, purposely seeking out the positive automatically reduces stress. Our brains have a tendency to focus on the things that are undone or out of place as a survival tool. Through retraining our thoughts we can see the good.

An example of this would be when we ask a child to clean the living room. When the child finishes, we inspect the completed job and immediately our eye goes to the one thing that is out of place instead of noticing the rest of the room that is nicely picked up. Rather than criticizing, we should look for the good, compliment it, and then invite a suggestion for improvement. The same is true when we are dealing with our own mistakes and imperfections.

<u>Fear of rejection/need for approval</u>—Basing our self-worth on what others think of us results in becoming overextended, mistreated by others, and even emotionally or physically abused. When our actions are based on what someone else thinks of us, we don't do things for the right reason. This causes high levels of internal stress, and can eventually lead to external symptoms of stress or anxiety. A fear of rejection by others, or a need for approval by others, is a distorted way of looking at life. While it is a blessing to have many loved ones and friends, there is ultimately only you and your Heavenly Father with whom you need to seek approval. Helping others can be a gift to others and ourselves, but always doing what others request leads to betraying our own feelings, values, and needs, It ultimately lowers self-worth and increases anxiety.

<u>Perfectionism</u>—Perfection is not expected, nor even possible in this life. When we insist on perfection from ourselves and others, we set ourselves up for disappointment. Perfectionism is an unhealthy expectation. Regardless of this, many good people beat themselves up when they fall short of it. Again, we need to focus on the process of life, what we are learning, and how we are progressing. We need to try our

best—not be perfect.

"What if" thinking—"What if" thinking is when our minds jump to the worst possible conclusion to any problem or situation that arises. It is a combination of several of the unhealthy thinking patterns we've already discussed. "What if" thinking blows things out of proportion, filters out the positive, focuses on a fear, and uses absolutes. "What if I don't pass the test?" "What if my child becomes a drug addict?" "What if I have anxiety again?" "What if I don't measure up?" "What if" thinking is a futile attempt to control the future. Instead of thinking "what if," we can tell ourselves to stay in the here and now. A good question to ask ourselves is, "What can I do now to control my thoughts and make positive decisions?"

"Should" thinking—"Should" thinking expects us to know or do things often beyond our ability at the time. It also compares our actions in the past with what would have been a better choice now that we know the outcome. Should thinking combines the hindsight we have now with guilt for not knowing better. It is a critical thinking pattern that doesn't change the past, but adds guilt and self-depreciation to our present state of being. A should statement sounds something like, "I should have invested in that stock when it was at $20." People who engage in "should" thinking have little patience with themselves. Accepting ourselves for who we are in the moment is one way to overcome should thinking.

Now that we've looked at the different kinds of unhealthy thinking patterns there are, let's discuss how to combat them. The first thing to do is identify which unhealthy pattern you slip into in times of stress. Think back to the most recent time you felt acute stress or anxiety. What was going on? What thought did you have right before you felt the anxiety hit you? If you can't remember what you were thinking, then you may have to wait for the next time you feel anxiety and then write down on a piece of paper that last thought you had right before you felt the anxious physical symptoms. These are trigger thoughts, and they are direct catalysts in contributing to the stress or anxiety we feel.

Once you have written down your trigger thoughts, refer back to the unhealthy thinking patterns we just discussed and see which ones are involved in the stress and anxiety producing thoughts you had.

Let's take Patricia for example. On Patricia's way to a staff meeting, all of a sudden her stomach feels a little upset. She recognizes the feeling as one she has when she is stressed, so she asks herself, "What was I just thinking?" As she thinks back, she remembers briefly thinking, "What if Doug presents right before me? It will make me sound like an idiot because Doug always sounds so good."

What unhealthy thinking patterns can be found in Patricia's trigger thought? Take a minute and see if you can identify any. Write them in the lines below.

____

____

____

____

Some of the obvious negative thinking patterns were: worrying solves problems, comparison thinking, and what if thinking. Some other patterns that may have been involved were: blowing things out of proportion, dwelling on the negative, and perfectionist thinking.

Try one more example. A woman with a newborn baby is trying to nurse for the first time. She doesn't seem to be able to get the baby to eat. The new mother starts to sweat and feel uncomfortable. Her arms start to tingle.

She recognizes these symptoms as signs of anxiety and asks herself, "What was I just thinking?" Taking a moment to reflect on her thoughts, she recalls saying to herself, "This is not working. I can't get my baby to eat. He is going to starve. I should be able to do this easily. Nobody else has a problem nursing their babies."

Try and identify the unhealthy thinking patterns in this mother's thoughts in the lines below.

____

____

____

____

What did you come up with? There were several unhealthy thinking patterns involved. For example: blowing things out of proportion, perfectionism, categorical thinking, comparison thinking, and "should" thinking.

The first step to changing negative thinking is to recognize unhealthy patterns. There are other negative thinking patterns than the ones we discussed, but these are some of the most common. As you look at the thoughts that produce stress in your life, you will be able to identify patterns that are involved with your thinking process.

The second step is to reverse and/or disprove these negative patterns. You can do this by trying the following exercises and techniques, many of which are based on cognitive therapy.

28. Change the Channel/Reframe/Re-script

Imagine yourself in the middle of watching your favorite television show. Suddenly, right in the best part, the image on the screen flips to a commercial. Each of us has experienced this scenario many times. What do you do? Some sit and endure the commercial, others pick up the remote and start changing the channel.

Unhealthy thoughts can be just like a commercial. We may be in the middle of something we really enjoy when all of a sudden unhealthy thoughts invade our mind. What can you do? First don't beat yourself up for having the thought. Tell yourself, "Hmm, there's that thought again. That's okay. I'm going to focus on something else."

Next, pick up your mental remote control and change the channel. It takes effort and practice, but it is possible. When an unhealthy or negative thought comes to mind, envision a remote control and push the channel button up or down, deciding beforehand on your next thought. While you can't stop an anxious even disturbing thought from entering your mind, you can change what your thoughts focus on. Recite your favorite quote. Mentally sing a song. Start thinking step-by-step what you are physically involved in such as a walking (i.e. "my foot is hitting the pavement and I am moving forward, propelled by my other leg"). Compose a story, or repeat some of your positive affirmations. Try to recall a fun day dream you may have or think of an enjoyable memory.

Knowing you are in charge of the next thought is an empowering feeling. Change the channel away from the negative thought. The negative or stressful thought may reappear, and that's all right. Just change the channel again. The more you practice at this, the better you will become.

Another way to deal with unhealthy thinking patterns is to reframe them. When you reframe a negative thought, you give it a good ending. For example, a negative statement from someone with insomnia might be: "Since I didn't sleep well last night, I'm going to have a miserable day today." Now let's try reframing that thought. For example, "I didn't sleep well last night. One time I didn't sleep well and I had a good day the next day because I gave myself a 30-minute break after lunch. Maybe I should do that again. Yes, that felt really good."

You can even reframe a thought by creating a fictional positive ending to a past negative experience. This is called re-scripting. Joyce was anxious driving home one night when her muscles started to twitch and spasm as a physical reaction to the tension she was feeling. On the ride home, the twitching became very bothersome, to the point that it compounded the stress and anxiety she was already feeling. In the next few days her muscle twitching got worse, especially when she thought of that drive home. Thoughts of that night would re-invoke anxious feelings in her. She decided to reframe her memory of that night with a better, fictional ending.

In her mind, she envisioned herself driving home and feeling the first few muscle spasms. Then, she envisioned seeing a duffle bag on the side of the road. She pulled over to retrieve the bag. Inside, she found it full of money. She noticed an address on the bag that was near where she was driving. She drove the bag to the address. She rang the doorbell, and a frantic woman opened the door. Relief spread on her face when she saw the duffle bag. Joyce handed her the bag and explained she had found it by the side of the road. The woman was so grateful she gave

Joyce a reward of $5,000 for returning the bag. Joyce then envisioned herself going to the mall and having a fantastic shopping spree, buying presents for everyone she loved, including herself.

Did she really find the bag? No, of course not. But the memory of the night when the muscle spasms began changed from a stressful, negative memory to one of enjoyment. By adding a positive ending to a thought or experience, you can put nagging, negative thoughts to rest and create positive thoughts and experiences in their place.

29. Do a "What Will Happen" Exercise

To do a "What Will Happen" exercise, chose a time in the day when you have fifteen minutes alone. Throughout the day you have hopefully been changing the channel on your negative, anxious thoughts. However, for the next few minutes you will allow your mind to dwell on what is giving you stress.

To begin, write the stressful thought you have been thinking at the top of a sheet of paper. Then, ask yourself the question, "What will happen if this is true?" Write your answer, which will probably be a heightened or deeper fearful event/response. Then ask yourself the same question, "What will happen if this is true?" Write your answer again. Continue asking yourself the same question each time you get an answer until your answer is the worst possible thing you can imagine. Most likely you have gotten to the root of the worry or stress.

Looking at your final answer, ask yourself a different question, "Could I handle it if this really happened?" Recognize you are not asking yourself, "Would I respond without stress or anxiety to this situation/response." Instead you ask yourself, "Could I handle it?" It may take work, pain, and patience, but could you do it?

Write your answer. Write down how you would get through it, and why you would do it. Write down resources you would use and positive things about yourself that would help you do it.

By doing a "What Will Happen" exercise (in an honest and reflective way), you accomplish several things. First, you find the root of your worry and you face it. Often, in doing a "What Will Happen" exercise we discover the dread of "something" is much worse than the "something" itself. Most people with stress and anxiety have such powerful, successful personality traits. These strong drives and high ideals can get them through problems successfully.

The following is an example of a real-life "What Will Happen" exercise from a client. As she entered a large store, she had the thought, "What if I have a panic attack in here?" This thought immediately started an anxious reaction, and even though she didn't have a panic attack, she felt uncomfortable. She decided to do a "What Will Happen" exercise right on the spot.

Original Negative/Unhealthy Thought: *What if I have a panic attack in the store?*

What will happen if this is true?

I'd be embarrassed. I would feel that I was out of control.

What will happen if this is true?
Well, that would be a reflection on me as a person, and it would mean that my life is chaotic and I am so incompetent I can't stop it.

What will happen if this is true?

I would feel that I am a flawed human being and a failure.

What will happen if this is true?

I will disappoint everyone in my life who is important to me.

What will happen if this is true?

That is it. I would disappoint everyone. That would be one of the worse things that could happen to me.

This was the woman's root fear. Now this individual asked herself this question: If I disappoint everyone in my life, could I handle it?

Right off I want to say NO! But that is not really true. I guess I could disappoint everyone—my kids, my husband, my parents, my friends. The only person that it really matters that I don't disappoint is God. But my anxiety doesn't disappoint God. He knows my physical weaknesses, and He knows how hard I try. In fact, the only way I could really disappoint God would be to choose to sin and then to choose not to repent. Other than that, there is nothing that would disappoint Him. That means, all I have to do in this store (the original negative thought*) is try and not commit sin while shopping, and that won't be hard to do. Whether or not I have a panic attack is unimportant, since that would never disappoint God. I can handle this.*

This “What Will Happen” exercise helped the person recognize she had an unhealthy mental pattern because she falsely believed she needed to have everyone’s approval. Facing that unhealthy thinking pattern helped her see the incorrectness of this belief, and it helped her see that if she did disappoint everyone because she had anxiety, she would still have value to herself and to her Heavenly Father. Doing this exercise took away the woman’s anxiety in the store, and it was a benefit to her in general as she better learned to manage her anxiety.

Doing multiple “What Will Happen” exercises about different anxious situations often reveals our specific fears boil down to one main fear.

30. Recognize Categorical vs. Abstract Thinking

Ryan was a hard worker and very successful, however, he couldn’t put down a project at work until it was complete. This meant he worked extra long hours, and often brought his work home with him. If he didn’t get the project done, then in his mind it was incomplete and he was not a success. If he wasn’t a success, that meant he must be a failure. This is categorical thinking and it results in stress or anxiety.

As mentioned before, we all think categorically as children, until the age of about eight. At this time, we begin thinking logically. At twelve, we typically begin abstract thinking, which allows us go beyond black and white thinking. Anxiety, stress, anger, and fear can cause or be a result of categorical thinking. As adults, categorical thinking is unhelpful because rarely is something all good or all bad. Gray areas are important to evaluate in abstract or process thinking.

If you are a categorical thinker, you can reprogram your thoughts to look at things as a process. One way to do this is to create a personalized satisfaction survey. After attending a conference, attendees are often handed a customer satisfaction survey to fill out. This survey typically asks if the conference was beneficial, what the person liked, what he or she didn't like, etc. How helpful would a customer satisfaction survey be if it asked only one question: "Was the conference good? Yes or No?" It would be useless. Instead, satisfaction surveys look for the progress made and where more improvement may be needed.

When you start thinking categorically about something, create a personal satisfaction survey instead. (Yours will change as the situation or category changes.) Use the survey provided below as an example.

Let's say you are feeling like a failure as a parent because of a conflict with a teenage child. You are not really a failure. That is a category. Instead, think of your relationship with that child as a process, and see where you are in that process. Decide what you're doing well, and what you could change.

Survey Concerning My Relationship with My Teenage Son

Not at all ____________________________________ Very Much

Do I love my son?

1 2 3 4 5 6 7 8 9 10

Have my son and I ever had a calm conversations?

1 2 3 4 5 6 7 8 9 10

Does my son know I love him?

1 2 3 4 5 6 7 8 9 10

Have I expressed my love to my son in the last month?

1 2 3 4 5 6 7 8 9 10

Has my son done anything positive for the family in the last month?

1 2 3 4 5 6 7 8 9 10

Are some of the conflicts I have with my son over unimportant issues?

1 2 3 4 5 6 7 8 9 10

How important is it to me to have my son close to the family?

1 2 3 4 5 6 7 8 9 10

Have I ever told my son this?

1 2 3 4 5 6 7 8 9 10

Have I been willing to come to a compromise once during the last month with my son?

1 2 3 4 5 6 7 8 9 10

This sort of a personal satisfaction survey will help you identify that you are not a failure, and it will also show you that you are not perfect. No one is! But it will show your strengths and where you could improve. Creating this sort of survey of a situation, helps you think more abstractly and view the challenge you are experiencing as a process.

As long as we are learning, we are not failures. If we are learning and moving forward, however slowly, we are progressing and improving.

31. Use Logical Thinking

Logical thinking is like having access to your very own personal detective agency. The logical side of your personality is the part that gets to the bottom of things, examines evidence, and forms logical, honest conclusions. Negative, anxious thoughts are rarely honest or logical.

The first rule of thumb is to never trust negative thoughts. When you find yourself thinking in unhealthy, negative ways, tap into your logical side. Ask yourself questions such as: "What are my symptoms? What was I thinking before my anxiety started? Why am I worrying about this? What I am really feeling?"

<u>Questions your logical side may want to ask:</u>

- What are my physical symptoms?
- What are my emotional symptoms?
- What are my mental symptoms?
- What are my spiritual symptoms?
- What was I thinking before my anxiety started?
- Can I identify a trigger (or several triggers) to this stress?
- Why am I worrying about this?
- What are my goals?
- What am I really feeling?
- What will my worry accomplish?
- What sort of unhealthy, negative thinking patterns can I identify in this worry?
- When did my worry begin?

After identifying what is really going on, a good detective would then move on to examining the evidence. Examine what sort of worry or stress you are having. Is there a technique in this book that may address this stress more directly than other techniques? What sort of evidence is there that directly refutes this worry? If you look at the worry or stress logically, what would you conclude about the truthfulness of it?

There are as many ways to examine the truthfulness of worries, stresses, and anxieties. No one idea fits every situation. Here are a few real-life examples of how people examined the evidence surrounding their stress.

Joan, a woman I worked with, decided to perform a pro/con analysis of why she often jumped to negative conclusions about the health of her children. This was her list:

Advantages of Jumping to Conclusions:

1. I know immediately the worst the future could bring.
2. I won't have any surprises.
3. When there are no surprises I am in control of the situation.
4. Jumping to conclusions gives me lots of time to prepare, and I like to feel prepared.
5. I like the feeling of having all my bases covered.

Disadvantages of Jumping to Conclusions:

1. While jumping to conclusions may help me feel like I will be more in control of external circumstances, it leaves me with less control of my internal feelings because it sparks anxiety in me.

2. Jumping to conclusions is mind consuming and often a waste of time because my worries and preparation for the worse possible scenario almost always go unused.
3. Jumping to conclusions fuels anxiety and leaves me physically worn out.
4. In the end, I'm fooling myself. I can't have all my bases covered in life. There are too many possible outcomes.
5. Jumping to conclusion sets me up for failure because it is humanly impossible to plan for everything and be in control of everything.

Joan was surprised to see all of the positives under why she liked jumping to conclusions. She was also impressed with the logical reasons she had discovered to not jump to conclusions. Her logical side helped her see that the pros of why she jumped to conclusions were fueling her unhealthy thinking pattern. After looking over the analysis, she decided the cons really did outweigh the pros. She would have to give up those things she liked on her pro list to prevent the cons from happening.

When her worries start, she now tells herself, "I know you like to feel prepared, but do you really want to waste all that time?" or "I know you don't like surprises, especially negative ones, but it is impossible to cover all your bases. You can move forward knowing you can tackle things as they come." Examining her worries logically helped Joan reverse an unhealthy negative thinking pattern.

Another example of a way to examine the evidence is to approach the situation as a scientist. One of my clients, Paul, was anxious over not being able to sleep well. Paul felt like a failure in that area.

He decided to examine the evidence by counting how many times he hadn't slept well over the past few years since he had experienced moderate anxiety. He knew on average he had one to two sleepless nights per months. During periods of high stress, the number increased to eight to ten days per month. He counted up all of the actual sleepless nights he had in the past few years. He then divided the number of total nights during that time period by the number of sleepless ones. He realized he slept well about 85 percent of the time. Anyone who has been to school knows that 85 percent is not failing! It is a B grade, and a B grade is actually above average. Looking at his stress logically helped Paul get over his thoughts about being a failure and relax enough to actually sleep better.

32. Reset Unrealistic Expectations

People who are stressed often feel overwhelmed. If you feel overwhelmed, you may need to reset your expectations. Sometimes, being overwhelmed has very little to do with how busy we are. Instead, it may have a lot to do with the expectations we have set for ourselves. For some Type A personalities, expectations are set at an unrealistic level of near perfection. . . in everything! We want our house to look a certain way. We want our children to be well-rounded and amazingly talented. We want our careers to be exciting and top-paying. We want to look like a super model. As expectations increase, so does the fear of failure.

To reset expectations, you have to be open and honest with yourself. Involving a spouse, mentor, friend, or counselor in this activity may be a good idea. Start by writing down some of the major things you actively participate in during the day.

The following list may help get you started:

- Personal appearance
- Business/work related projects
- Meals
- Social life
- Personal health
- Health of family members
- Involvement with children's school
- Civic/community responsibilities
- Church responsibilities
- Children's appearance
- Children's extra-curricular activities
- Appearance of home (inside and out)
- Appearance of car
- ____________________
- ____________________
- ____________________
- ____________________
- ____________________
- ____________________

Next, list what you want to see happen with each of these activities. You may find you are expecting too much. With another person's help, decide which things are not as important *to you* as other things. Expectations are a personal matter and no two people are the same. You may decide having a perfectly clean home is not going to help you achieve any of your main goals in life. This may be an area where you can reset expectations. For example, you could reset your expectations to having a clean entrance way and living room every day and cleaning bedrooms and the rest of the house as a family on Saturdays. That means during the week you don't have to scurry around cleaning the entire house.

Another person may decide that spending hours in the kitchen cooking and cleaning isn't that important. To someone else, having at least one hot meal a day as a family is important, which means that person will have to organize the schedule to fit that priority. Another person may decide attending every nighttime meeting isn't necessary. A solution might be to set a quota for the number of nighttime meetings allowed each week.

After resetting expectations to match your daily activities, write them down and post them where you can see them. When you start to feel overwhelmed, look at your expectations and see if you have fallen back into the habit of expecting too much.

33. Weed out the Non-Essential

Some of us simply have too much to do every day. This often stems from the inability to say no. For others, it may stem from not seeing the difference between essential and non-essential activities. Here are a few real-life examples.

One woman was spending a lot of time on the phone for social calls. At least an hour or two of her day was spent talking on the phone to friends. She decided she needed to limit herself to five minutes every time there was a social phone call. After five minutes, she told the caller that she had to go. She allowed herself longer conversations on the phone if she was involved with activities where she could talk and work such as mopping the kitchen floor and weeding the flower beds. This one change in her schedule saved her hours per week and reduced her stress of feeling overburdened.

One easy-to-learn technique to saying “no” is setting quotas. We have already talked a little about this in the section on resetting expectations, but let’s discuss it a little more. A well-run business will set up quotas for its employees or an allotment for its customers. Why not do something similar in your personal life? For example, you may need to set a quota on the number of babysitting favors you do a month. Perhaps it is the number of volunteer projects you take on. Once your quota is full, you know you have to say no to any more requests for that month or week (or however you set up the quota). The more committed you are to your quota, the easier it is to say no with a smile because *you* aren’t really the bad guy anymore—you are sticking to your goals and nurturing yourself.

We often try to reduce our stress by involving ourselves in non-essential activities (i.e. video games, television, or movies). And although some of these may help us unwind, too much may leave us feeling empty and unsatisfied. Rejuvenating activities are those that build us up; those things that add to our knowledge, health or relationships to other people.

It is about finding a balance. The balance must be between helping and loving others and caring for our needs, or loving ourselves. We cannot neglect ourselves without affecting our ability to help others. Anything we take care of we value more, including ourselves.

Non-essential and essential activities fill up each of our lives. But, with a little monitoring of your day, you may pinpoint some areas where a lot of your time is going. One man, after reviewing his daily activities, realized he spent very little time building relationships with his wife, which happened to be one of his main goals. He rearranged his schedule and set up some quotas so he could go on regular date with his wife every week. Changes such as this give us a peace of mind that the important things in life are truly a priority.

34. Look Forward to the Future

Having chronic stress or anxiety diminishes our desires to daydream or think about the future in a positive way. Retraining our minds to think about wonderful, exciting activities can increase our hope for the future and help us feel better. Children do a great job at creating wonderful dreams and hopes. One boy created an entire fantasy land he could go to when upset. It had a waterfall with soda pop and flowers of chocolate and cream. The animals could talk to him and he could run faster and jump higher when he was there. He used this fantasy when he needed to calm down. He felt better when he went to his personal place.

A great way to regain our desire to daydream and lessen anxiety is to plan positive future activities. This is also a great method to use when you are mentally changing the channel. When a negative thought enters your mind, change the channel to the event you are planning and go over the details in your mind.

In the beginning, you may dread the idea of planning a fun, positive activity. However, the more you do it, the more you will feel like it is a natural thing to do again. Start small. For example, plan a special dinner for your family. Plan a picnic. Plan to do a surprise in your spouse's lunch. Use the list of self-rejuvenating activities if you can't come up with some on your own, and plan a surprise evening for you and a friend, a spouse, or for your entire family. Looking forward to the future and positive events is an important part of managing stress and anxiety and reversing unhealthy thinking patterns.

In the movie, *Auntie Mame* (1958), there is a line that reflects how most of us are creatures of habit. When we get into a rut in our daily lives, we need to push ourselves to explore exciting, new territory. The line from the movie states, "Life is a smorgasbord and most poor suckers are starving to death!"

Don't limit your happiness by avoiding new experiences or stifling creative hobbies? Create a joyful future for yourself by stepping outside of your comfort zone and partaking of life's smorgasbord.

Willing to Change

There is story about a stream that flowed through the mountains, foothills, and meadows, feeding the grass and trees along the way. The stream flowed around many obstacles until it finally arrived at a desert. The stream tried to cross the desert, but its waters evaporated into the hot, dry sand.

The stream cried out in fear and anger, "Why can I not cross the sand?"

It heard a voice say back, "The wind crosses the desert. So can the stream."

The stream answered back, "The wind can fly, but I am not like the wind."

The voice gently replied, "Let the wind absorb you and carry you aloft."

The stream protested, "I want to remain the same stream that I am today."

The voice urged the stream on saying, “You’ve forgotten from whence you have come. Your essence can be carried in the wind, across the desert as it once was.”

The stream let her water rise into the vapor that was carried in the arms of the wind. Across the desert she flew and the wind let her fall into the mountains where she became part of an even larger, more beautiful stream.[39]

Instead of telling yourself you have to stay the same person you’ve always been, allow challenges to mold you into a new person. As you experience stress and anxiety, you will grow. Do what you can to manage your stress and anxiety and then accept yourself. Don’t feel ashamed to have this trial. Consider yourself a student who is auditing a class about stress. You get the learning without having to worry about the grade. When you feel stress or anxiety, approach it as a learning experience. After it has passed, review what you did well, and what you could improve. Remember, there are no failures. It is only a process!

The opposite of accepting your stress or anxiety and growing from it is to run away from it, deny it, or fear it. All of these attitudes actually invoke more stress and more anxiety.

Psychologist and author Reid Wilson explains, “Here is the paradox: to win against panic you must stop fighting it or running away from it.”[40]

I remember a time in my life when I had to learn to let go and try and change my way of thinking in response to a very stressful situation I was experiencing. My business partner and I owned a mental health clinic that often took on interns from local colleges to train them to be therapists. We had taken a young man studying to be a psychologist into the clinic. He had done an internship for us for over a year when he admitted to his supervisor he had been sexually involved with a client. We were horrified.

The woman who was involved decided to sue him and the clinic. I met with the woman and offered counseling and gave her assurance that we wanted to try and do what was right. The law suit continued. I could not continue doing therapy with the fear of losing my business, home, and license to practice. I couldn't give the energy, care, and strength to others if I was not whole.

As I was faced with having my license and livelihood taken away and never being able to help others in that capacity again, I felt incredible stress. I knew I had to change my way of thinking because it was destroying me. I had to do what I could do, and then turn the rest over to the Lord.

I prayed to God and asked Him to take my burden. I would do what I could, but I had to turn over the fear, worry, and problem to Him. From that moment on, I put no negative energy into the law suit. Over the next three months, we sent records to attorneys and cooperated all we could. All that time, I trusted that the only one that could solve this problem was God. After about three months, we received a letter saying that the law suit had been dropped. The Lord had taken care of one of the greatest fears I, as a psychologist, have experienced.

The young man involved divorced his wife, lost custody of his children, and could never become a therapist. He was also excommunicated from the LDS Church. Shortly afterward, he moved out of state. More than four years later I met the man again in a most interesting place and way. I was in the celestial room in the Oakland temple. This young man came through the veil with his bishop. It was the first time he had been to the temple since being reinstated in the church, and there I was, one of the first people who greeted him in the celestial room of the temple.

He had been able to turn his life around as well, and I felt joy with him at his success. I had no ill will toward him. Since I had changed my way of thinking about the problem, I hadn't experienced any lasting pain. The Lord had taken it away. It was a blessing for me to see what the Lord could accomplish when we are willing to change.

CHAPTER SIX—Tools to Strengthen Your Spiritual Health

The Brother of Jared is the *Book of Mormon* prophet who had enough faith to see the finger of Jesus Christ. But that was not always the case. After escaping the Tower of Babel, the Brother of Jared led his family and friends by following the Lord hidden in a cloud to the edge of the wilderness where the ocean began. Once he reached the ocean front, however, the Brother of Jared stops seeking the Lord. For four years "he remembered not to call upon the name of the Lord" (Ether 2:14).

Why did he stop communicating with the Lord? Since the scriptures don't tell us why, we can only speculate. Could it be that the Brother of Jared had some anxiety about crossing the ocean? Imagine having no Global Positioning System, no map, and no clue as to what existed at the other side of the ocean. Would you have some anxiety about jumping in a dark, windowless boat? The four years camped by the ocean front were a spiritually low time for the Brother of Jared, and most likely a very anxious time as well.

Did the Lord forsake the Brother of Jared because of his fears? No.

God came to the Brother of Jared and gave upon him another chance. "And the Brother of Jared repented of the evil which he had done, and did call upon the name of the Lord" (Ether 2:14). As the Brother of Jared works through the details of crossing the ocean in a barge, he also overcomes some of his fears. The Lord allows the Brother of Jared to come up with his own ideas on how to light the dark vessels. In the process, the Brother of Jared reduces his fears and grows in faith, so much so that the Lord tells him that "never has man come before me with such exceeding faith as thou hast" (Ether 3:9).

The Need for Spirituality

In the scriptures it is easy to find those who have trials because of their sins—Laman and Lemuel from the *Book of Mormon* and the traitor Judas from the *New Testament* just to name a few. However, we forget that good people like the Brother of Jared also have trials. Sometimes these trials are self-inflicted because we don't listen to the Lord, like when Martin Harris lost one hundred and sixteen pages of the first translation of the Book of Mormon (D&C 3:10). Other times they are inflicted by others, such as when Nephi was bound by his brothers during their voyage across the sea (1 Nephi 7:16). And sometimes bad things happen that are no one's fault, such as when Christ explains to His disciples why a particular man had been blind from birth: "Neither hath this man sinned, nor his parents: but that the works of God should be made manifest in him" (John 9:3).

Christ is the ultimate example of trials happening to good people. Elder Yoshihiko Kikuchi, a former member of the Quorum of the Seventy, said, "[Jesus] faced a state of loneliness, agony, disappointment, denial, desertion, extreme mental and physical, even emotional stress which caused him fear on fear."[41] We too face challenges that threaten not only our physical, emotional, and mental health, but our spiritual health as well.

Doctors and mental health professionals often ignore or are timid about discussing a person's spiritual health. Yet when physical or mental health declines, both religious and non-religious people report they hunger for some form of strengthened spirituality. A poll in *Newsweek* magazine showed that 72 percent of Americans said they would welcome a conversation with their physicians about faith. The very same number say they believe praying to God can cure someone.[42] Our spiritual side is an integral part of who we all are.

Strengthening our spiritual dimension is essential when healing from emotional and mental trauma. However, sometimes spiritual interventions may not be as effective when the other dimensions—physical, emotional, and mental—are still ill. The Lord himself said, "See that all these things are done in wisdom and order; for it is not requisite that a man should run faster than he has strength… therefore, all things must be done in order" (Mosiah 4:27).

Elder James E. Faust, a member of the Quorum of the Twelve, said:

> "The healing that we all so often need is the healing of our souls and spirits. This can come through a transfusion of the spiritual into our lives. The seventh article of faith states that, among other spiritual gifts, we believe in the gift of healing. To me, this gift extends to the healing of both the body and the spirit. The Holy Spirit speaks peace to the soul, and this spiritual solace comes by invoking spiritual gifts, which are claimed and manifested in many ways. They are rich, full, and abundant in

> the Church today. They flow from the humble and proper use of a testimony. Christ is the Great Physician who rose from the dead with healing in his wings (2 Nephi 25:13), and the Comforter is the agent of healing."[43]

In this chapter, we will discuss ways to strengthen our spiritual dimensions. As you read over the ideas in this chapter, recognize that you can ask your Father in Heaven to help you know what will bring you the greatest peace of mind and strength of spirit. The techniques in this chapter are, as the old adage says, "stars to steer by, not sticks to beat ourselves with." As you listen to the spirit, it will guide you in manageable, specific ways to find health and healing.

Why Suffering?

Suffering is a universal thread that binds us together. Whether we live in a three-story house with jetted tubs, or in a hut with a thatched roof, challenges will come. There is ample proof from history that good people have problems, stress, and even tragedies. The world is also full of hope, healings, and miracles. Spirituality helps us make order of seemingly random events in life.

Years before there were pink ribbons and monthly self-exams, my mother found a large lump in her left breast. She was a healthy woman just entering her mid 50s. When her doctor saw the lump, he told her to go to the hospital immediately. An examination revealed she had invasive breast cancer and the decision was made to operate the next day.

The lessons she learned during this time have given me a clear focus as I have experienced my own challenges. My mother, now in her 90s, taught what it means to have trust and faith in a loving Father in Heaven. This is her story:

After the operation, I was returned to my shared hospital room where a woman occupied the second bed. As I lay quietly that evening, I began to pray, expressing my desire to live yet voicing my trust in the eventual outcome. Suddenly, I felt I was lifted up into a glorious, brilliant white light. My feeling was that of incredible peace. I remained as quiet as I could so as not to disturb the woman in the bed next to me who was having surgery the next day.

The next morning my roommate turned to me and said, 'Did you feel the earthquake last night?' I replied, 'No.' She continued, 'On your side of the room everything was shaking.' She had seen the miracle I experienced.

Two years later, I went to see my surgeon for a check-up. At this time he finally told me, 'I did not think you would ever make it because the cancer had gone into all the lymph glands on the left side.' I give thanks for my life.

My mother's suffering brought her a faith in God that has spanned decades.

Karla, a client, came to me for counseling during a difficult pregnancy she was experiencing. At the beginning of her visit, I asked her if there had been a purpose to her suffering during the pregnancy before this one. Immediately she responded, "Yes! I have my little girl."

"Good," I said, "as you enter this new pregnancy, you can tell yourself with confidence that there is purpose to this suffering." By recognizing that suffering has purpose, we can greatly reduced our stress from it. A common human trait is the ability to bear things if we know there is a purpose.

Some difficulties, however, may last years before their purposes are realized. When we strengthen our spiritual health, we live peacefully not knowing what the purpose to our suffering is, but having faith that it is there.

Listening to the Spirit

Sometimes our spiritual dimension becomes sick when we refuse or forget to listen to the spirit's promptings. Lack of attention to our inner voice and the good things around us may leave us empty. Another cause of spiritual disconnection is when our actions contradict what we believe to be true.

Spiritual carelessness can happen to anyone. I remember once I was working out in the garden. I noticed a bottle of weed killer my husband had left on a brick ledge along the driveway by our lawn. Several times I passed the bottle as I was working outside. Each time I did, I felt an impression to move the bottle and put it away. Every time I felt the impression I dismissed it, thinking I would do it later. As I walked by the bottle the last time the same feeling come over me, but I didn't act on it. Then, just as I turned around to go into the house, our German shepherd, Rooster, came through the door and ran by the bottle, knocking it over with her tail. The bottle broke and the poison ran all over the lawn and driveway. The lawn never recovered from the strong dose of poison it received that day.

Spiritual strength and listening to the spirit helps our bodies and minds stay strong. One study showed that people who regularly attend church have a 25 percent reduction in mortality.[44] Scientific research supports the power of combining spiritual healing with other areas of healing. Scientists studied two groups of Christian clients with depression and anxiety. The first group was given standard therapy. The second group was given religiously oriented therapy. The largest absolute reduction in depression and anxiety was from the group of Christians given the religiously oriented therapy.[45] Strengthening our spiritual dimension is essential when seeking physical, emotional, *and* mental healing.

Doing Our Part

Another important principle to remember is that "faith without works is dead" (James 2:26). By only focusing on spiritual healing and ignoring the body's other dimensions, we stall the healing process. Just like some people ignore the spiritual side to healing, others ignore the physical, emotional, and mental aspects and become frustrated that their faith hasn't healed them. A complete approach is really the best and most effectively way to effectively manage stress and anxiety.

Many years ago when my husband was a young missionary serving in a third world country, he became very ill after mistakenly drinking the water. He had severe diarrhea for a week, and he went to the doctor. He received various medicines and took them as directed, yet his illness continued. At this point, he turned to the Lord.

> *After about two weeks of trying several medicines to no avail, I gave up. I thought I could just live with it. As the days continued, however, I started losing my strength and I became*

anxious about my condition. I could no longer peddle my bike and I could hardly even walk. Feeling the despair of my condition, I knelt in prayer. I poured my heart out to God.

While praying I saw a scene unfold as if a video were playing in my mind. At the top of the hill, I saw a street vendor selling fruits and vegetables. I knew I must hurry to find this man and purchase two green apples from him. I got up and started for the top of the hill.

I could barely make it to the top of the hill, but when I finally did, the vendor was there. I asked his pardon for delaying his return home, but asked if I could purchase two green apples. He accommodated my request. I ate the apples and before the end of the day my condition was reversed at last.

By doing our part and then relying on faith to make up the rest, we can find healing to anxieties and physical concerns.

Spiritual Management Techniques

35. Understand Guilt

When we have guilty feelings or experience emotional pain, it could mean one of two things—our actions are in conflict with what our inner voice tells us is true or our understanding or view of the matter is incorrect (a distorted belief).

A young woman who had been married for seven years came into my office. She was experiencing marital problems. Her husband was demanding her to perform sexual acts she was not comfortable doing.

When she told him no, he became upset with her. She could no longer live with the way she felt, and she came to counseling to seek help.

As she spoke of her pain and emotional upheaval, I was impressed to ask her if her husband was addicted to pornography. She said he could never do such a thing. I explained to her that normal passions and desires can be pushed into addictions if we stimulate them beyond normal bounds.

I felt inspired to ask her to talk with her husband and invite him to the next session. A week passed and I saw the young woman again in my office. This time her husband was with her. She had talked with him, and to his credit he admitted his addiction to pornography. He had been struggling with it for years, even before their marriage. Their marriage had been a stressful one because his actions went against what the spirit told him was right. His guilt, from an incorrect action, eventually led him to seek help and change. With treatment, his addiction was overcome and the marriage improved.

On the other hand, I know another man who lost his job and for nearly a full year was unemployed. After several months in this situation, he felt stress, guilt, and shame that he couldn't provide for his family. As his anxiety increased, he began to question his spirituality. He told himself that if he was more spiritual, God would provide him a job.

Was this man's guilt from actions that went against his inner voice or was it from a distorted view that God must be punishing him since he couldn't get a job? He had forgotten that even good people experience hard challenges. There is purpose to suffering. After nearly a year of unemployment, his efforts paid off. He found a job that worked better with his family's schedule and paid him more than his previous employment.

Many times when good people feel stress or anxiety, they automatically assume that in some way they are not measuring up. They worry about what they are doing to incur God's wrath. When we mentally distort our culpability, we lose sight of goodness and truth. We put more pressure on ourselves and in so doing increase our stress or anxiety.

Elder Alexander Morrison, an Emeritus member of the Quorum of the Seventy, spoke of emotional and mental health saying, "It must be emphasized that in many instances aberrant thoughts, actions, and feelings result from mental illness and not from sin. The truth is that many faithful Latter-day Saints, who live the commandments, and honor their covenants, experience personal struggles with mental illness."[46]

Guilt, from incorrectly inflicting shame and inappropriate responsibility upon ourselves, can negatively affect our lives and our health. One psychologist who studied the religious coping methods of patients with chronic illness found that those ill patients who thought God was punishing them or abandoning them were up to 30 percent more likely to die over the next two years.[47] Assuming that all problems, trials, and stress are God's way of punishing us is distorted. In actuality, God has said:

> "And if men come unto me I will show unto them their weakness. I give unto men weakness that they may be humble; and my grace is sufficient for all men that humble themselves before me; for if they humble themselves before me, and have faith in me, then will I make weak things become strong unto them" (Ether 12: 27).

There is a wonderful story of two monks walking by a river observing their vow of silence during the day. The river was overflowing, and a young woman in a silk dress stood by the bank, terrified. She asked the monks for help, and the first monk picked her up in his arms and carried her across the river. The two monks then continued walking in silence until sunset. As the sun set, the second monk turned to the first.

"How could you have picked up that woman?" he sputtered angrily. "You know very well that we are prohibited from even thinking about women, let alone touching them. You sullied your honor."

"Dear brother," replied the first monk, "I put that woman down on the other side of the river at sunrise. It is you who have been carrying her around all day."[48]

Carrying shame and guilt within us creates destructive feelings that feed anxiety. We must learn, as the first monk did, to "put down" whatever it is that is bothering us and continue on. If we carry distorted guilt around with us, our spirituality suffers. If we carry true guilt around we also suffer. Instead, we can find stillness by 1) changing our actions that are in conflict with the gospel and the promptings of the spirit, and 2) stopping self-deprecating thoughts and forgiving ourselves.

36. Distinguish Between Inspiration and Fear

When people are stressed and anxious it can be hard to interpret feelings clearly. Beth would often awaken in the night having a panic attack. She recounted her confusion at these times because she didn't know if the fear she felt was the Holy Ghost telling her to get her children out of the house because something bad was going to happen to them, or if what she was feeling was part of her anxiety.

For Beth, it was difficult to distinguish between anxiety and warnings from the Holy Ghost.

This is a common concern for those with anxiety. When in the throws of feeling panic, it is important to remember, "God hath not given us the spirit of fear; but of power, and of love, and of a sound mind" (2 Timothy 1:7). Since Beth felt confused and fearful, it was a good indication these feelings of fear were not inspiration, but the result of the anxiety. If the spirit were telling her to get out of the house, it would be a clear message that resulted in swift action, not panic.

I learned this very lesson myself years ago. I remember receiving a letter from my son who was serving as a missionary in Germany. The winters there were cold and rainy. The wind and moisture penetrated normal overcoats. In his letter, he asked me to send to him his fleece-lined jacket as soon as possible. He didn't remember exactly where it was, but he assured me it was at home somewhere.

I began the search for his jacket. I looked everywhere. I checked closets, drawers, boxes, under beds, in the garage, and in all the nooks and crannies of the house. After a week of frantic searching, I still hadn't found the jacket. I knew I needed to find it quickly or go purchase a new one.

During my last effort looking for the jacket, I realized for a week I had been listening to my fearful, frantic, stressful voice. Not the whisperings of the spirit. I decided to calm down about finding the jacket and seek quiet inspiration. I prayed and meditated. When I felt peaceful, I felt ready to listen.

I started walking around the house, and as I headed towards my son's room I had the frantic thought slip in, "Maybe I should check once more in his room." The way the thought came into my mind I knew this was stress talking. I tried to clear my mind and follow the peaceful promptings. As I walked around the house once more, I found myself in front of the door to the garage. This time my thought was, "No, my husband already checked there." I recognized this thought as my own intrusive thought, as it came with anxiety not peace.

So I followed the feeling to enter the garage. I walked around the cluttered garage and was lead to a pile of boxes stacked on top of one another. I took the top boxes off of the bottom ones. Without looking in them, I reached into the bottom of the biggest.

I felt the soft, fleece-lined jacket and pulled it out. For an entire week I had listened to frantic, stressful thoughts and had little success. Three minutes after calming myself, I had found the jacket. While this experience is about a simple jacket, I learned from it a huge lesson. As we learn to quiet our anxiety and listen to the inspiration of the spirit, we can learn to distinguish between inspiration and fear.

37. Redefine How You Feel God's Love

A person who is anxious or stressed may feel he or she has become numb to spiritual feelings. It is like trying to listen to a radio station plagued with static. When our physical bodies are under duress, it can be difficult to feel God's love. However, as we strengthen our "reception" by looking after our physical bodies, our spiritual channel will become clearer. In addition, we may need to redefine the way we feel the love and acceptance of our Heavenly Father.

From the scriptures we learn that God's love feels like peace, joy, and happiness. When someone is under chronic stress, these emotions may be difficult to feel. Consequently, the person may wrongly conclude God no longer loves him or her.

Trudy was successful at so many things in life, yet at times she suffered from depression and anxiety. During one of her anxious moments, she expressed that it must be her punishment in life to never feel the love of God. That is a very lonely way to exist! Even though she didn't feel God's love in her life, it was there. She was an amazing gardener, piano player, and mother. She was patient and kind. She had a gentleness about her that spoke of an inner goodness in her soul. God did love her, but when she was anxious she didn't know how to feel it.

In Galatians 5:22 and 23 it says, "But the fruit of the Spirit is love, joy, peace, longsuffering, gentleness, goodness, faith, meekness, temperance." The first of these three fruits are common: love, joy, and peace. We've already talked about those.

Let's take a look at some of the others fruits of the spirit such as longsuffering. Are you gentle with your children even when inside you feel turmoil? If you are, that is longsuffering and it is a gift of the spirit. Have you maintained your faith during hardships? If so, that is faith, and it is another fruit of the spirit. The ability to be meek, or willing to ask your Father in Heaven for help, is another fruit of the spirit. These are often manifestations of the spirit and God's love that we overlook.

The following list contains some fruits of the spirit gleaned from the scriptures and other church writings that are not as obvious as the fruits of love, peace, and happiness but are just as important.

Fruits of the Spirit

Ability to love others

Clarity of thought

Compassion

Determination

Faith

Gentleness

Gift to be healed	Goodness
Gratitude	Knowledge
Longsuffering	Meekness
Pricked in the heart	Satisfaction
Temperance	Testimony
United feelings	Whisperings

Look for these and other manifestations of God's love for you. President Heber J. Grand said, "We should thoroughly understand that in no single day or hour of our lives would we be able to stand alone and maintain the testimony of the Gospel without the light and inspiration of the Spirit of God."[49]

38. Pray and Fast

The physical act of praying has been proven to be successful in relaxing both the body and the brain.[50] Physiological responses to prayer include a slower metabolism, a slower heart rate, and lower blood pressure. Even a person's cholesterol levels may drop. Physically the amygdala slows down its hyper-vigilance in detecting danger, and higher ordered thinking skills in the frontal lobes of the brain engage.

A study done at the Virginia Commonwealth University Medical College of Virginia in Richmond studied one thousand nine hundred and two twins. They found that individuals who were committed to their spiritual lives and prayer tended to have less severe depression and a lower risk of addiction to cigarettes or alcohol than their twin sibling.[51]

Latter-day Saints know that prayer is effective because it is communication with our Heavenly Father who knows the present, past, and future. He understands what we need more than we do.

Those who already take the time to meditate or pray daily, may find that the experience begins to lack sincerity or effectiveness when it becomes dull or tedious. Those who are anxious and stressed, may have difficulties slowing down their thoughts to invoke sincere prayer. Whatever the reason, it may be helpful to review the basics of prayer.

Some think of prayer only as something to do at certain times of the day—before a meal or going to bed. While this may be true, a deeper understanding of prayer shows it can also be an attitude—a way of thinking.

Prayer is remembering God in your daily activities. Muslims teach this through their greetings and expressions. When a fellow Muslim sees another Muslim, he does not simply wish him a "Good day." Instead, the expression is, "May the peace of God be with you."

President Ezra Taft Benson said this about prayer and mental health:

> "Prayer in the hour of need is a great boon. From simple trials to our Gethsemane, prayer—persistent prayer—can put us in touch with God, our greatest source of comfort and counsel. 'Pray always, that you may come off conqueror' (D&C 10:5). 'Exerting all my powers to call upon God to deliver me' is how the young Joseph Smith describes the method that he used in the Sacred Grove to keep the adversary from destroying him (JS—H 1:16). This is also a key to use in keeping depression from destroying us."[52]

Here are some ideas to infuse more meaning into praying:

- Pray in a different place or at a different time of day. When your surroundings change so may your thoughts.
- If you know another language, pray in it instead of your native tongue. This will use the higher ordered thinking areas of your brain, and it will engage deep thinking.
- Try writing down your prayer and then listening to your thoughts and feelings.
- Pray by saying and thinking nothing—only breathe deeply and try and feel your environment around you. This type of prayer is especially effective when surrounded by nature.
- Pray as if you are having a conversation with a dearly loved, wise old grandparent who knows your ins and outs.
- Try a prayer of gratitude only saying or thinking things for which you are grateful.
- Ask for something specific in a prayer.
- Find a quiet place free from distraction.
- Acknowledge intrusive thoughts you may have while praying and let them pass through your mind. Don't hang onto them and don't get upset at yourself for having them.

I challenge clients who are suffering from chronic stress and anxiety to pray and ask God if they are loved and to help them understand their purpose in life. During times of anxiety, one of the most beneficial things you can ask in a prayer is, "What can I learn from this trial?" Prayer takes faith, willingness to hear what God has to say, and obedience to what we are told.

On a hot Californian summer morning (the forecast predicted temperatures of 109 degrees Fahrenheit), I was rushing to finish my hour-long, daily ritual of watering the trees, bushes, flowers, and vegetables. As I finished the first fruit trees, the water stopped flowing from the hose. I ran to the well and checked to see if the pump had stopped. I attempted to reset it. No luck. I still had no water. I checked the power, reset buttons, and did everything else I knew how. Nothing worked. I was getting more and more upset with each attempt to solve the problem.

As I was frantically trying to find out how to fix my problem, I came to many dead ends. I finally looked skyward and asked in a frustrated voice, "Am I suppose to learn something from this?"

My sarcastic question was answered with a calm, but physically forceful feeling of, "Yes." It stopped me in my tracks. I felt stupid and ashamed for my bad attitude.

"Okay," I said to myself, "if I'm supposed to learn something from this, I'd better calm down and pay attention."

I walked over to my horses to check if they had enough water in their troughs and was shocked to find my prize brood mare swollen up and covered with hives. She was having difficulty breathing, and her eyes were swollen shut. She had evidently gotten into some fly bait that had blown into her corral in the night. I immediately called the veterinarian, who arrived at the same time as the repair man for the pump. The horse and pump were fixed within the hour. If the well hadn't stopped pumping, I would have never checked my mare, and she would have died.

As we ask what we need to learn or discover from a trial, it fosters an attitude of humility and learning. As we seek to know what we need to learn from a stressful experience, we will find that in the learning we better manage the anxiety or stress because now it has a purpose.

Many years back I had another experience with prayer that taught me the importance of asking. I had a free hour and decided to go out into the garden to weed. The day was hot and dry in the month of August, and the red, clay soil was like cement. I started pulling the sticky weeds from the ground. They cut my hands and broke off without the roots.

After thirty minutes, I began complaining aloud: "I'm trying to do something good. I need to clear the weeds so our dogs won't get burrs in their skin. Could you help me out here?"

As I was complaining, I received this answer in my head, "You are upset with me for not helping with your weeding, but you took no thought to ask me in prayer before you started your task. When you pray, and your prayers are answered, you can acknowledge my influence in your life and my love for you. When you do not pray, you take the glory to yourself and I cannot bless your life or show my love for you." Upon receiving this guidance, I prayed for help and was able to complete my weeding with wonderful results. But more importantly, I learned the importance of not being too proud or frustrated to ask.

Elder Robert D. Hales of the Quorum of the Twelve Apostles said:

> "There is nothing that we are enduring that Jesus does not understand, and He waits for us to go to our Heavenly Father in prayer. I testify that if we will be obedient and if we are diligent, our prayers will be answered, our problems will diminish, our fears will dissipate, light will come upon us, the darkness of despair will be dispersed, and we will be close to the Lord and feel of His love."[53]

In addition to praying, fasting is an effective way to clear the mind and strengthen ourselves spiritually. We our counseled to not take it to extremes, but when done with the right spirit it is a powerful tool in healing the mind and soul. Regular fasting reminds us of our commitment to the Lord and His gospel. Many of my clients have added fasting to their stress management plans and felt a great difference in their ability to calm themselves.

> "And when they were come to the multitude, there came to him a *certain* man, kneeling down to him, and saying, 'Lord, have mercy on my son: for he is lunatic, and sore vexed: for ofttimes he falleth into the fire, and oft into the water.
>
> 'And I brought him to thy disciples, and they could not cure him.'
>
> Then Jesus answered and said, 'O faithless and perverse generation, how long shall I be with you? How long shall I suffer you? Bring him hither to me.'
>
> And Jesus rebuked the devil; and he departed out of him: and the child was cured from that very hour.
>
> Then came the disciples to Jesus apart, and said, 'Why could not we cast him out?'
>
> And Jesus said unto them, 'Because of your unbelief: for verily I say unto you, if ye have faith as a grain of mustard seed, ye

> shall say unto this mountain, remove hence to yonder place; and it shall remove; and nothing shall be impossible unto you. Howbeit this kind goeth not out but by prayer and fasting' "
> (Matt. 17: 14-21).

It is during times of fasting and prayer when many are blessed with powerful answers. I remember one time in particular when I had been doing a special fast. I was tired, and I had a nap. During the nap I had a vivid dream. It involved me having to protect a book. This book was very special, but I had lost it when I set it down to get an ice cream cone (one of my weaknesses). I knew I had to get the book back, and I spent the rest of the dream facing peril, danger, and evil getting the book back.

When I awoke, I pondered the meaning of the dream and realized it answered some questions I had been having. I knew I had shown great faith in the dream. I knew I had a testimony of Christ, and that my testimony was a blessing to me and others. I shouldn't let innocent distractions of the world keep me from my eternal purposes. Lastly, I knew I was personally worthy to be helped and guided in those things I needed to accomplish. The dream was so vivid that it stayed with me for several days. Fasting truly is one way in which we humble ourselves and open ourselves to God's miracles and blessings.

Elizabeth had been dealing with stressful months of illness, impossible deadlines at work, and other personal issues. She felt completely exhausted. She was having disturbing physical symptoms associated with anxiety. After consulting with her doctor, she felt she needed to go on medication to help manage the anxiety. However, the medication would not take effect for several weeks, and she knew she needed strength now.

So she turned to her family. She asked members of her family to fast for her on an upcoming Sunday. In her own prayers and fasting, she didn't ask that the anxiety be taken from her. Instead, she asked for strength to make it through until the medication could take effect. That Sunday morning she was still not feeling well. She had not been able to sleep and she felt dissociated and panicky. Regardless, she attended church during which her husband invited a couple over to share dessert with them that evening.

She hoped she would feel strong enough not to burst out crying during this couple's visit. As Sunday wore on, she became increasingly worried about the evening. When the couple arrived, however, something happened. For months she had felt her strength and peace of mind was draining from her. However, as she received her guests she felt for the first time in months like someone was pouring strength back into her body. It wasn't all at once, but as the evening progressed her peace of mind began to return. She knew it was from the fasting and prayers.

By the end of the evening, she knew she would make it through this hard time in her life. She knew the fasting and prayers of others had set her on the road to getting better.

39. Seek Answers in the Scriptures and the Temple

We have so many media choices. We need not settle for the ordinary. One way to calm ourselves and find reassurance is by seeking words of faith that strengthen weak knees and remind us we are not alone. The time to read the latest thriller novel is not when stress and anxiety are high. Instead, reassuring, motivating, and positive literature, especially the scriptures, helps the mind and body relax, especially the scriptures.

Spiritual leader Mahatma Gandhi (1869-1948) said:

> "When doubts haunt me, when disappointments stare me in the face, and when I see not one ray of light on the horizon, I turn to the *Bhagavad-Gita* (Hindu scripture), and find a verse to comfort me; and I immediately begin to smile in the midst of overwhelming sorrow. My life has been full of tragedies and if they have not left any visible and indelible effect on me, I owe it to the teachings of the *Bhagavad-Gita.*"[54]

Our own prophet, Ezra Taft Benson, said, "Many a man in his hour of trial has turned to the *Book of Mormon* and been enlightened, enlivened, and comforted."[55]

Words of inspiration can be anchors in our lives. One experience in particular taught me to turn to uplifting reading in times of unrest. My family was faced with a move to California. No one but my husband was excited to go. I loved our home, neighbors, schools, and friends where we were, and yet I wanted to support my husband in his work. We took many trips to California to try to find a home there. All of our attempts to find a place failed. I was beginning to wonder if moving was the right thing to do.

I was anxious about moving, and I dreaded looking for a home. Each time we searched, I became more concerned and discouraged. One night while I was reading, I turned randomly to a page in the Bible. It opened to John 14: 1-3:

> "Let not your heart be troubled: ye believe in God, believe also in me. In my Father's house are many mansions: if it were not

> so, I would have told you. I go to prepare a place for you. And if I go and prepare a place for you, I will come again, and receive you unto myself; that where I am, there ye may be also."

The words in the passage took on new meaning for me, and I knew that our family would be fine, and we would find a home where we would be happy.

As we read the scriptures looking for answers, we will find we can learn from the trials of others and how they were strengthened. From the scriptures we learn about patience, determination, faith, and trust. Most importantly, we learn to trust our Savior by learning of His life, His miracles, and His love through His sacrifices for us.

In addition to the scriptures, temples are wonderful places to find inspiration in challenging times. Beginning with the Ark of the Covenant in the *Old Testament* to the modern restoration of temples by Joseph Smith, we have been taught that temples are a powerful source of strength and peace.

During the dedicatory prayer of the Kirtland temple, Joseph Smith prayed, "And we ask thee, Holy Father, that thy servants may go forth from this house armed with thy power, and that thy name may be upon them, and thy glory be round about them, and thine angels have charge over them" (D&C 109:22).

Our modern prophets and apostles have confirmed the importance and power behind the temple. Elder Boyd K. Packer said:

> "No work is more of a protection to this church than temple work and the genealogical research that supports it. No work is more spiritually refining. No work we do gives us more power.

> No work requires a higher standard of righteousness. Our labors in the temple cover us with a shield and a protection, both individually and as a people."[56]

Prophets have promised that as we make the temple an important part of our lives, peace and power will enter our hearts and minds.

Mindy was in her early thirties, yet doctors told her she was beginning menopause. In conjunction with the drop in hormone levels she was experiencing, she felt anxious. She decided it may be helpful for her to try some sort of meditation.

During one of her meditations, she tried to visualize herself in the celestial room of the Provo, Utah temple. She thought this would be a serene, peaceful place on which her mind could focus. Each time she tried to visualize the celestial room, however, she found her mind wandering to the temple's front waiting room. She visualized herself sitting on the couch feeling sorry for herself because of her problems. She thought to herself, "I am a woman with hormone problems. What does my Savior know about that? Does he even understand what I am going through as a woman?"

At this moment in her meditation, she heard a voice that said two words, "Look up." There, on the wall in the waiting room of the temple right in front of her was a large, beautiful painting of Jesus and the woman at the well. Tears swelled in Mindy's eyes. She knew the Lord understood her troubles, just as he understood the troubles of the woman at the well.

In whatever way we can, we should incorporate the temple into our lives. In doing so, we will find added strength and insight in managing stress, fear, and anxiety.

40. Give Service

Imagine the scene. It is the early 1980s and the Israelis and Palestinians are in the midst of a military skirmish. The streets are empty since people fear they might get caught in the crossfire. During the middle of this highly charged situation, a 72-year-old woman, a catholic nun, is able to persuade the leaders of both groups to declare a cease fire. During the cease fire, the woman known as Mother Teresa rescues thirty-seven mentally handicapped patients from a besieged hospital in Beirut. How did Mother Teresa have the peace of mind to do what she did? She said it was because when she served others she forgot her own anxieties.

In doing service, we are blessed to worry less for ourselves and find compassion in the depths of our souls for others. Elder Marvin J. Ashton said:

> "If we love Him, we will feed His sheep wherever they may be found, without regard as to our own personal plight or situation. Often we can best feed others when we are hungry ourselves or not completely comfortable in the fold that we presently occupy. Very often those who are hungry, helpless, and cold can best be rescued by those who have been through the same exposures. There is a healing power as we use our energy in action, in service, and in lifting others."[57]

Angie was having a particularly stressful day. She was feeling a pit in her stomach, and couldn't seem to relax. Her thoughts centered on her demanding schedule. During her drive home, she noticed a neighbor's large garbage can had fallen over, spilling garbage on the road. As she drove by, she realized her neighbor would have a hard time cleaning up the mess because of a physical disability.

She knew what she had to do. She stopped the car, backed up, and got out. She spent a few minutes gathering the spilled garbage, and then she set the can upright. She got back in her car and headed home again. As she reached her driveway, she realized her thoughts from before the garbage can experience to after the garbage can had completely changed their focus. Earlier, her thoughts had been about herself. After picking up the garbage, her thoughts were about her neighbor, his plight, and how good she felt to have done something for someone else. She had experienced a universal truth: when we serve others we serve ourselves.

When my children were young, they had a very hard time on fast Sundays. They thought about their empty stomachs and complained or constantly asked when they could eat. My husband and I decided to distract them from their discomfort by doing something for others on fast Sundays.

Each fast Sunday, we baked a batch of cookies. All of us would pray about who should receive the cookies. We tried to think of those in our neighborhood or ward who were having trials or sickness. We would then package up the cookies and sneak over to the family's home we had chosen. We would try to leave the cookies on the doorstep without being caught. It was so exciting to the children that they forgot their own hunger while planning how to surprise someone else. Many a fast Sunday we were spent hiding in bushes, being chased by dogs, or running furiously to remain undetected. As a family, we truly learned how service lifted our own lives and lightened our burdens.

There is an old Hassidic story about a Rabbi who is explaining to a group of children the difference between heaven and hell.

"Heaven," he says, "is like sitting at a large table, surrounded by people you know, with every kind of food you love on the table. The only problem is your elbows won't bend."

"Hell," he continues, "is also like sitting at a large table, surrounded by people you know, with every kind of food you love on the table. Once again, your elbows can't bend."

"So what is the difference between heaven and hell?" the children ask.

"In heaven," the Rabbi answers, "the people feed each other." So it is when we serve others.

41. Work for Forgiveness

Forgiveness is much like service. When we focus less on our own grief and more on things outside of ourselves, we shed worries and anxieties. President Spencer W. Kimball taught, "The essence. . . of forgiveness is that it brings peace to the previously anxious, restless, frustrated, perhaps tormented soul."[58]

Some members of the Church understand the doctrine of forgiveness to mean that we should not feel offended or simply ignore grievances. This is not healthy. If we ignore or internalize pain caused by the mistreatment or abuse of others, we can damage ourselves both emotionally and physically.

Our emotional state deeply impacts our nervous system and in turn our nervous system is intricately linked to our immune system. In fact, our nervous system is what tells the immune system what kind of immune response the body needs. It is for this reason that some autoimmune disorders such as lupus are connected to or at least triggered by emotional trauma.[59]

Scientists who study psychoneuroimmunology (the link between the body's nervous and immune systems) have found that even common physical ailments such as allergies and eczema are found more often in people with anxiety and are often triggered by an internalized stress.[60]

Honesty is crucial in forgiveness. Even though perpetrators of an injury may deny the injustice, the offended should do his or her best at releasing feelings (verbally or in written form). When possible, it is healing to let the offender know how we were offended. In some serious situations of offense, this is not possible or would cause more abuse and retaliation. In these cases, feelings can be released to a trusted friend, mental health professional, or spiritual leader.

Only when feelings are acknowledged, expressed and released can forgiveness be possible. One woman shared the following story with me on how she came to forgive her husband:

> *There was a time in my life when I honestly did not know if I could cope. Life had many changes, and my dear grandmother, to whom I was very close, passed away. Before her death, she told me during an emotional goodbye that she would always look out for me.*
>
> *The year after her death proved to be filled with obstacles for me and my husband. We had been struggling to make a connection for several months. I did not know what to do or why it was happening, but I felt that I had lost my best friend.*
>
> *I will never forget the morning I was getting ready for the day when I heard my Grandma's voice speak to me as if she were in*

the room. Her words were, "Mary, you need to go ask Steve if he has had an affair" I went and posed the question to my husband. He answered, "Yes." I felt my world crumble beneath me.

Through much patience, love, understanding, and forgiveness, my husband and I have been able to rebuild our relationship. We are once again best friends, companions, and lovers. Once there was honesty, we could begin the healing process.

Once we have recognized our pain and admitted that an offense hurt, it is time to ask ourselves, "How can I respond to this pain? Do I want to let this pain take root and grow, or do I want to rid myself of it?" If we truly want to rid ourselves of the pain, then we must turn to the atonement of Christ for the gift of forgiveness. This comes through prayer, fasting, temple worship, scripture reading, and serving others.

Keep in mind that forgiveness may not be a single event. For some offensives, forgiveness may be a long, difficult process. It may require fervent and repetitive attempts, and possibly the help of family or a trusted spiritual leader. Eventually, the goal of forgiveness is to be able to distinguish between the individual and the individual's offensive and hurtful actions.

As a psychologist, some of the most powerful experiences I witness in therapy are apology sessions between a perpetrator and an abused individual.

When a perpetrator is genuinely sorrowful for his or her actions and apologizes for how he or she has hurt another, there is a wonderful healing process that occurs for both individuals. Although a genuine apology doesn't take away the pain of the abuse or the physical and emotional damage created, it can validate the abused individual's innocence and suffering. Heart-felt apologies can begin the healing process and allow for eventual closure.

Unfortunately, apologies are often not available from perpetrators. Amazingly, the efforts of forgiveness on the part of the abused individual can bring about the same healing and closure for him or her, even without the apology of the perpetrator. I believe this is one of our Heavenly Father's kindest mercies.

42. Change Perfectionistic Thinking

Kate was a young girl who was having trouble in school. She was a brilliant child and knew most of the curriculum the teacher presented, but she was failing. Every time she tried to do a homework assignment, if it wasn't perfect she would throw away the paper and start over. Homework often took her all evening and many times she refused to turn it in if it wasn't perfect. Her need to be a perfect student was causing anxiety in her life and in her parent's lives.

I worked with Kate to help her better manage her perfectionism. We discussed the fact that some of the most valuable art and tapestries were those with imperfections. Machines can duplicate art with perfection, but the human touch adds a quality and uniqueness that cannot be duplicated. Simple mistakes and imperfections are what make some things of greater worth.

Kate worked on allowing herself to be human and in using honest self-reflection to determine if her efforts were acceptable. Truly, all of us are a "work in progress." Kate was teachable, and she learned to accept mistakes and feel good about her work. Her grades improved, and her anxiety decreased.

Not getting upset over imperfections is a powerful way to manage stress and anxiety. However, to some members of the church this concepts seems contrary to Christ's teachings in the *New Testament* where He says, "Be ye therefore perfect, even as your Father which is in heaven is perfect" (Matthew 5:48).

This scripture is a beautiful request for us to follow the example of our Savior and Heavenly Father. Unfortunately, this invitation to join our Savior in eternal life with Heavenly Father is misinterpreted to mean live our lives here on earth perfectly. The footnote associated with this verse in the LDS scripture explains that the Greek word translated as "perfect" in the current King James Bible means "complete, finished, fully developed."

When will we be "complete, finished, and fully developed?" Not on this earth. Elder Bruce R. McConkie explained:

> "Nobody becomes perfect in this life. Only the Lord Jesus attained that state, and he had an advantage that none of us has. He was the Son of God, and he came into this life with a spiritual capacity and a talent and an inheritance that exceeded beyond all comprehension what any of the rest of us was born with.
>
> He lived a perfect life, and he set an ideal example. This shows that we can strive and go forward toward that goal, but no other mortal—not the greatest prophets nor the mightiest apostles nor any of the righteous saints of any of the ages—has ever been perfect, but we must become perfect to gain a celestial inheritance. Becoming perfect in Christ is a process.

> As members of the church, if we chart a course leading to eternal life; if we begin the processes of spiritual rebirth, and are going in the right direction; if we chart a course of sanctifying our souls, and degree by degree are going in that direction; … then it is absolutely guaranteed—there is no question whatever about it—we shall gain eternal life."[61]

When we feel the need for perfectionism, we can remind ourselves that perfection in an imperfect world is not possible. Instead, we can seek to learn from the process of life and find enjoyment and understanding along the way.

43. Believe in Miracles

Miracles are gifts. They strengthen and uplift in times of need and stress. Miracles can be quietly at work in our lives, so much that they may seem like coincidences. Miracles can also be powerful acts of healing or change—so significant that we can't deny them. As I meet with hundreds of people in therapy, almost everyone has experienced miracles. Miracles strengthen a believing heart and bring peace to the anxious soul. Look for them in your own life.

One woman shared this miraculous story with me:

> *I was diving off the shores of California with some friends. I had suffered from a cold a week before, but I felt mostly better. I had taken some medicine to be sure. As I was diving, I felt a very sharp pain in my chest. It made me gasp and I lost the regulator out of my mouth. I remember thinking, 'This is how it feels to drown. I am going to die!'*

I felt strangely peaceful as I looked up at the bubbles of air floating to the surface. I began sinking in the deep water, but I felt serene. I felt I was in a very sacred place but that I needed to go back for my children. I then remember an angel putting the regulator back in my mouth and getting the first few breaths of air. I started the assent with the angel guiding me back to the surface. As I reached the top of the water, my chest hurt so badly.

My diving companions helped me, and I was taken in a helicopter at the lowest altitude possible. I was taken to the Catalina Dive Chamber and placed in the decompression chamber for over ten hours. After my treatment there, I was flown to the Los Angeles County Hospital for further treatment. Over the next two months, I had two treatments a day. I went to a neurologist for several months after the incident. I was told that I was the first person in fifteen years to live through this type of accident.

They found that the medicine I had taken had created a bubble in the mucus in my sinuses. As I ascended, the bubble expanded and blew a hole in one of my lungs. The air in the blood went right to my brain, causing a stroke on my left side. Miraculously, I fully recovered. It has been thirteen years since the accident.

Another woman recounted to me a miracle in her life that was a much more subtle, but a miracle just the same.

I had a toddler and a young baby. We were in the middle of a move, and it was a very stressful time in my life. I was helping load all of our belongings into waiting trucks. The mattresses and bed frames were leaning on their sides against the master bedroom wall. My baby was lying on a blanket on the floor in the master bedroom. As I scurried out of the room carrying a bag, I had the thought, "Pick up your baby.

Almost without thinking, I shifted the bag to one side, leaned down, and picked up my infant. As I exited the room, the movement from walking out the bedroom door caused the mattresses and bed frames to fall to the floor, exactly where my baby had been. Only then did I realize that the thought to pick up my baby had been a prompting—my own small miracle.

There are various ways to invite miracles into our lives. Having faith in a God that loves us and cares about us is the first place to start. We must practice listening to the spirit, and we must learn to trust ourselves to act upon what we hear. Lastly, when miracles do happen, we need to show gratitude. Being grateful is the final stage in a miracle and it is the part that will change us, not just the miracle itself.

44. Live a Good Life

When one of my children was two years old, for Christmas we purchased a motor scooter that could propel him around the house. My husband and I were sure he was going to love it. We were so excited for his reaction on Christmas morning. When the time finally arrived to unwrap the gifts, my son ran to the Christmas tree. He pushed the smaller presents aside and went right to the large, brightly wrapped gift that contained the scooter. We were thrilled he chose the one we knew he would love.

He promptly played with the present's ribbon and shinny paper. We encouraged him to open the gift and rip the paper off, but it took quite a lot of convincing. Finally the ribbon and paper were removed and the large brown box was revealed. So, my son then started playing with the box. He jumped on it, stood on it, but didn't open it. We again coached him to open the box. At last the scooter was revealed. My husband and I raved over it, but my son decided to play hide and seek in the brown box instead of noticing the gift.

How similar is this incident to our attempts at finding happiness in life? How many of us play with life's wrappers and boxes and never get to the intended gift inside? When we live a good life, we unburden ourselves from telling ourselves what we should be doing. Instead, we are content with what we are doing.

But how do we live a good life? Unfortunately there is no set formula. Our lives will each be different and unique. However, I believe the techniques in this book will help. It is hard to mistreat family and friends if one is meditating each day and serving others. It is unlikely that you will berate yourself or others if you are performing positive affirmation and recognizing unhealthy patterns of thinking.

Chances are we will prioritize well if we have a focus on our main goals in life and we journal regularly to keep track of our accomplishments. Whatever areas you focus on, they will lead you to living a better life.

The most important part of living a good life is making the atonement of Jesus Christ a priority.

Sister Kathleen Hughes, former first counselor in the Relief Society General Presidency, said:

> "I have learned from my own experience that we are never left to our own resources. We are never abandoned. A wellspring of goodness, of strength and confidence is within us, and when we listen with a feeling of trust, we are raised up. We are healed. We not only survive, but we love life. We laugh; we enjoy; we go forward with faith.
>
> The living water also nourishes. I testify to you that just as He promises, Christ comes to all who are heavy laden; He gives us rest (see Matt. 11:28). He sustains us when we are weary. A wellspring is a flowing well, offering continual refreshment—if we drink of it."[62]

There is no substitute for the Atonement of Christ. As we seek to strengthen our spiritual dimension, we have increased peace and stillness in our souls.

Be Still

One dark December evening I was boarding an airplane headed for home. It was the holiday season and my family had already arrived at my home in California ahead of me. I couldn't wait to see them. It was snowing and the weather reports said the storm would continue through the next afternoon. By the time I was on the plane, the snow was a white blanket covering the ground, and a blizzard raged in the freezing cold night.

Inside the plane, the cabin was frigid. The flight attendant passed out blankets to the passengers, but there were not enough to go around. The plane had to be de-iced. The pilot turned the engine off, and the de-icing process seemed to take forever. The snow kept getting thicker and deeper outside, and the cabin was getting colder inside.

I began praying that we could make it out. The captain came over the speaker and stated that now the engine was frozen and it had to be de-iced too. He said if the weather kept up, we would need to return to the terminal.

At this particular time in my life, it felt very important to me to get home for Christmas. I kept repeating in my mind the plea, "Please let me get home. Please let me get home."

The plea started to consume my thinking. I could feel my anxiety levels rise. I wanted so badly for the blizzard to stop long enough for the plane to get off the ground.

After several minutes of my frenzied pleading, I finally stopped my mind's chatter to listen. And there, in my thoughts, rang the gentle, quiet words from Psalm 46:10, "Be still and know that I am God."

Immediately the worry ceased. I calmed myself, and recognized that I was not the one in charge. It is moments like these, when we finally acknowledge a higher power at work in our lives, that true faith is born.

Incredibly, the moment after my fears calmed, I looked out the window to see the blizzard slow down, thin out, and stop altogether. Within a minute, the sky was clear overhead. The pilot announced we would take off. We taxied down the runway and as the plane was pulling up into the sky, the snow began once again to fall. I would be home for Christmas.

A promise made by the Lord is found in the *Doctrine in Covenants* where it says: "Let us cheerfully do all things that lie in our power; and then *may we stand still*, with the utmost assurance, to see the salvation of God, and for his arm to be revealed" (D&C 123:17).

My experience on the plane that day taught me that whatever may be the circumstance, we can face it with courage, dignity, and most importantly, stillness.

APPENDIX A—More Ideas for Religiously Oriented Therapy

Researchers studied two groups of Christian clients with depression and anxiety. The first group was given standard therapy. The second group was given religiously oriented therapy. The largest reduction in depression and anxiety was from the group of Christians given the religiously oriented therapy.[63]

So what is religiously oriented therapy for a Latter-day Saint? The following is a short list of secular techniques that incorporate religious practices to increase and expand healing.

- If you are trying to manage stress through better nutrition, follow the guidelines in the Word of Wisdom, and refer back to it when you find yourself overeating unhealthy foods.
- Make the scriptures or *Ensign* part of your non-stimulating reading material you may need at night to help insomnia.
- When setting goals, don't forget spiritual goals such as temple worship.
- Prayer is an excellent form of meditation.

- When doing visualization, try envisioning spiritual images: the temple, temple grounds, heaven, or our Savior with outstretched arms.
- Read the scriptures outside, attend the temple, listen to religious music, or participate in a religious activity (i.e. fireside) as part of your self-rejuvenating activities.
- For journaling, try writing down your testimony or a prayer.
- When trying to connect with your child-like self, you may want to visualize the *New Testament* scene when the Savior calls the little children to Him.
- As part of your personal relationships, draw upon your visiting teachers and home teachers.
- Write a list of the things God would say about you for positive affirmation.
- When you change the channel, change it to a spiritual preconceived thought—maybe your favorite scripture memorized, or a phrase from your patriarchal blessing.
- Search the scriptures for examples of continuous vs. categorical thinking, accepting weaknesses, or examples of others managing stress.

There are many ways to incorporate gospel concepts into a stress and anxiety management plan. Learn what secular techniques work best for you, and then try increasing their effectiveness by integrating a spiritual image, concept, or principle into the technique.

APPENDIX B—For Parents of Children with Anxiety

Childhood fears are normal, and a natural part of growing up. They appear and disappear during different times in a child's life. While childhood fears are normal and real, at times these fears and anxieties can turn disruptive. In fact, it is estimated that one in ten children have a moderate to severe problem with anxiety.[64] When deciding if your child's fears have turned extreme, ask yourself these questions:

- Is my child's anxiety seriously affecting his life?
- Is my child's anxiety a problem for her?
- Does it interfere with activities he used to enjoy?
- Do his anxieties stop him from doing normal childhood things?
- Is it affecting her in academic or extra-curricular activities?
- Are my child's fears disrupting our family?

If you answer "yes" to several of these, you may want to implement some stress and anxiety management techniques into your child's life.

Some Characteristics of Anxious Children

Anxious children often have one or more anxious parents. Anxiety runs in families. Other characteristics of anxious children may include:

- They may avoid certain situations like dark places or social situations.
- They may be hyperactive and aroused from excess adrenaline.
- They may be shy and have a limited number of friends.
- They may do well on homework but poorly on tests.
- They may fidget, pace, cling, and cry more often than other children.
- They may have academic problems at school, not because they lack intelligence but because their desire for perfectionism is actually negative.
- They often have thoughts that center around some type of danger or threat.
- They tend to be more emotional or sensitive than other children. This means they are likely to be more naturally caring, charitable, kind, honest, obedient, and loving than others. They are also more fearful, worried, and easily upset.

The way parents react to a child's anxiety may help to reduce or aggravate the anxiety. Many times parents react in an overprotective way to a child's anxiety. This is especially true of parents who struggle with anxiety themselves. Parents may try to protect their child from an anxiety provoking situation and in so doing, never the let child "face the fear." If a child never has to face the fear, soon he or she may develop the notion that the fear really was justified. Anxiety in children is often kept alive by running away from frightening situations. If you take away every uncomfortable situation from your child, he or she continues to run away. Instead, prepare your child for an anxious situation the best you can, and then allow the child to work through it on his or her own. Remain a resource to the child, but don't overprotect the child if there is no real danger present.

Parents may also give too much attention to a child when he or she acts anxious. This attention is actually a reward, and it tells the child that this negative behavior earns positive results. It is much better to teach stress-reducing skills to your child. Then, when the anxiety appears, empathize with your child and express confidence in his or her ability to resolve the problem using the skills he or she has learned.

In addition to being careful with your response to your child's anxiety, there are other things you can do to help an anxious child manage his or her stress more effectively. Most, if not all the techniques in this book work for children as well as adults. However, some may be more effective and easily achievable with children than others. The following are some effective ways to help manage stress and anxiety in children.

Methods Effective for Children

1. <u>Regularly express confidence</u> in your child's ability to manage stress in a good, constructive way.

2. As a parent, <u>model calm behavior</u>. Your behavior greatly influences your children's behavior. If you model calm behavior, you will find your children will try and follow your lead. Think back to your days in elementary school. Did you ever have a teacher that would whisper when

the children got too noisy? Soon, the children would follow suit. If you remain calm in stressful situations, children are more likely to follow suit.

3. Set up routines and structure, especially at nighttime when anxiety for children tends to increase. Set consistent bedtimes, homework times, special music for bedtime, etc. Establishing healthy routines gives children a sense of security and positive self worth. Imagine living in a world where you never get to say when you are going to the store, when you can play, what clothes to wear, etc. The more control you give your children with simple tasks, the better they may feel about things in their life over which they have no control.

4. Encourage realistic thinking. We know that events can trigger beliefs and thoughts, and beliefs and thoughts lead to feelings. We can't control events, but we can control beliefs and thoughts. Unrealistic thoughts precede anxiety. To help your child learn realistic thinking, you must first identify the unrealistic thoughts that precede his or her anxiety. For children, these thoughts often exaggerate a bad outcome. Teach them to look for the evidence of what is really going on inside his or her thoughts. You may even tell your child to pretend he or she is a detective looking for the facts. To find out the facts, ask questions such as:

- What was I thinking before I began to worry?
- Have I worried about this before?
- What happened when I was worried before?
- What are the facts about my worry?
- What are some good outcomes that could happen?

- What is a more positive thought I could have?
- What do I think will really happen from this situation?

These questions will help your child see his or her unrealistic thought that came before the worry. It will also remind them that the last time he or she had this fear (and faced it) everything turned out OK. These questions help come up with alternative things to think about, and help the child conclude that realistically, the outcome doesn't have to be bad.

5. Practice social skills with your child. A lot of children have anxieties with social situations. A good way to overcome these anxieties is following the adage practice makes perfect. Practicing social skills can be fun and beneficial. Make a game out of it, and offer rewards for a job well done. Some skills you could practice with your child may include:

- how to answer a question
- how to ask a simple question
- how to ask for help
- how to handle teasing
- inviting others to play or participate
- looking people in the eye, but not staring
- picking topics to talk about in public
- saying hello
- shaking hands
- smiling
- standing and not fidgeting
- sticking up for him or herself
- talking at a moderate speed (not too fast)
- talking in a voice loud and strong enough to hear

6. Help your child express emotion. Some children may not know the name of the emotion they are feeling when they are anxious. Being able to express emotions is an important step in teaching your child how to recognize stress and worry. Explain what worrying feels like, and help your child pinpoint physical characteristics he or she feels when worry is present. You may want to decide between one and ten how strong the worry may be. For younger children, you may want to draw faces that visually express emotions such as relaxed, sad, angry, disappointed, and worried. Under each face, help your child write the type of emotion that face is feeling. Use these face drawings later to help your child identify the worried emotion when he or she is having anxiety.

A game that the whole family can play is called the jelly bean game. In this game, a person takes a bag of jelly beans (preferably one with many different and interesting colors) and pulls one out without looking. He or she has to name the emotion the jelly bean reminds him or her of, and then name a time in the last few months that he or she felt that way. Every member of the family takes a turn. This game helps children learn how to identify and express emotions.

7. Teach your child to relax. There are many ways for a child to relax. They can learn abdominal breathing, muscle tension relaxation, and visualization. One of the most effective ways of relaxation for children is through massage. Research on the importance of touch has been acknowledged for many decades. Nurturing massage has been used with infants, children, and adults as a successful tool to lower stress and create emotional comfort.[65]

It is best to practice massage with your child regularly, but not necessarily when he or she is anxious, since you don't want to be rewarding anxious behavior. For massage to be relaxing to your child, plan for at least 15 minutes of time with your child without distractions. Often the best times are when the child is relaxed in the morning or before bed.

Before beginning, be sure to let the child know that if you do anything that is uncomfortable he or she should immediately tell you. Let the child know that he or she is in complete control.

Choose one target area with the child. It could be the face, back, legs and feet, or arms and hands. Good smelling lotion or oil can be used to help moisturize the skin and allow for a more comforting experience. Use the following instructions for the different target areas you choose.

> Face: Rub along the forehead, and circle the temples. Move over the bridge of the noise and under the eyes. Circle the cheeks and rub along the jaw line. Lightly touch your child's face, starting with the forehead, over the eyes, cheeks, and chin.
>
> Back: Move in a circular motion at the base of the neck and over the shoulders. Next, start at the top of the spine and work outward toward the shoulder blades and down toward the lower back. Allow the child to determine the amount of pressure to use.
>
> Arms and Hands: Start with the fingers and move in a circular motion. Work the palms and outer hands. Follow the hand bones on the outside of the hand and use circular motions around the wrists. Massage muscles in the arms to the elbow.
>
> Legs and Feet: Start with the toes. Use the same circular motion

as you did with the hands. Massage upward on the outside of the feet. Use the side of the hand to make long strokes on the foot arch. Pinch the heel softly, and circle the ankle bone. Use long firm strokes on the legs moving upward toward the knee. Gently circle the kneecap.

These exercises can be very beneficial with infants and children in increasing serotonin levels. It also helps you bond with your child.

8. Help children make choices for themselves. Some children can't make choices without it creating stress and anxiety. My son at the age of four had difficulty every time we went to the store to choose a treat. He would stand for a long time in front of the candy counter picking one treat and then putting it back and crying until it made him sick. We decided that he needed to make the decision about what candy he wanted before he arrived at the store, when he wasn't faced with so many choices.

An hour or so before we left for the store he would think about his favorite type of candy and choose one. Then, when he got to the store, we would remind him of his choice and congratulate him on doing so well. We would also let him know he would have many more opportunities to choose a treat. Next time he could try another favorite one. He was able to overcome his anxiety by choosing ahead of time when the pressure of too many choices was not present.

Another way to help children with choices is to narrow the field. Give children two outfits they can choose from to wear, instead of an entire closet. It helps to build their confidence without overwhelming them.

Seek Help When Needed

As parents, we often perceive our children as small appendages to ourselves. We falsely believe that if the appendage is not doing well, it reflects our own inabilities. This attitude stops many parents from seeking professional help with their children. Just like adults, however, children can benefit by discussing their anxieties and fears with a trusted counselor. If a child's anxious behavior continues for an extended period of time and increases instead of decreases with time, it may be helpful to seek professional help. Typically counseling is effective in children ages four and older.

Sarah and Jim were at a loss about what to do with their son. He was a smart, active child, but his fears were affecting the entire family's well being. In the evenings he would cry for hours about the possibility of getting a cavity. He had seen a film at school about dental hygiene, and since that time he had obsessed about brushing his teeth. These episodes became more frequent and longer. His siblings teased him, and his parents were frustrated.

After several months of this behavior, Sarah and Jim took their son to counseling. During counseling they learned their reaction to their son's behavior was not as effective as it could be. They learned how to express confidence in their son's ability and strength. They were assured they were good parents, and that this behavior was common in high strung children at this particular age. Their son learned about anxiety in understandable terms, and he learned things he could do to manage it better. The frustration and anxious behavior their son exhibited greatly improved after seeking professional help.

APPENDIX C—For Victims of Physical, Emotional, and Sexual Abuse

There is a link between abuse as a child and anxiety as an adult. If you or someone you know has been physically, emotionally, or sexually abused, there may be some facts to consider.

To begin, child abuse is real. Sadly, children are more likely to be victims of abuse in their own homes than on the streets. According to the U.S. Department of Health and Human Services, every year 3.3 million reports of child abuse are made in the United States involving nearly six million children.[66] Most experts agree that the number of reported cases of child abuse is only a fraction of the actual number.

A survey of adolescent boys revealed that one in eight high school boys reported being physically and/or sexually abused. Additionally, 48 percent of physically or sexually abused boys said they had not talked to anyone about their abuse.[67] One in five high school girls surveyed reported being physically or sexually abused, and 65 percent of those girls said the abuse happened more than once. The findings showed 29 percent of girls who had been physically or sexually abused had not told anyone about the abuse.[68]

These same surveys found that 46 percent of abused girls had symptoms of depression, which is more than twice the rate of girls who said they had not been abused. Results showed abused girls have double the risk for developing an eating disorder. While numbers do vary, some research indicates that an abused child has four times the risk of developing anxiety or depression as an adult when compared to adults not abused as children.

Latter-day Saint children are at risk like the rest of the world. The *Ensign* reported:

> "Unfortunately, not even Latter-day Saint homes are free of this stain. President Gordon B. Hinckley has expressed his indignation: 'There appears to be a plague of child abuse spreading across the world. …I am glad there is a hue and cry going up against this terrible evil, too much of which is found among our own.' "[69]

Being abused as a child is not a life sentence for emotional or mental difficulties as an adult. The above statistics demonstrate only that child abuse is real, and that it must be dealt with whether as a child or as an adult. We should not minimize its presence in our society, but we should also not maximize its affect on our success and desire to live a happy life.

We should believe children when they reveal abuse and react calmly. It is my experience that children rarely make up stories about being abused. In fact, one child who had been sexually abused talked with me about her confusion over anyone who could think she made up the abuse. She innocently stated, "I could never have thought up anything as yucky as that in my whole life."

President Gordon B. Hinckley has said abuse is contrary to the teachings of the gospel, and that the perpetrator of abuse is guilty for the wrongdoing, not the victim.

> "The terrible, vicious practice of sexual abuse… is an affront to the decency that ought to exist in every man and woman. It is a violation of that which is sacred and divine. It is destructive in the lives of children. It is reprehensible, and worthy of the most severe condemnation.
>
> Shame on any man or woman who would sexually abuse a child. In doing so, the abuser not only does the most serious kind of injury. He or she also stands condemned before the Lord."[70]

All human beings suffer painful experiences, and some of these experiences occur in childhood. Someone may have had a childhood illness that deeply affected his or her life. Someone else may have had to experience the death of a loved one such as a parent at a young age. Being abused as a child is not the only painful and potentially hurtful experience that human beings may suffer in childhood. Everyone has to find his or her own way to cope with emotions caused by painful experiences in life.

The after effects of abuse are varied because the type, length, and level of abuse differ from child to child. If an abused child had other avenues of love and support, the abuse experienced may not be as deeply rooted. Some of the other factors that may contribute to how a person responds to abuse is whether or not secrecy behind the abuse is maintained for a long time. Another factor is if the child had relationships in which expressing feelings and emotions were acceptable. Other factors include how close the abuser was to the child emotionally (i.e. a parent or sibling vs. a stranger), and the duration and intensity of the abuse.

Recognize that not all abused children have difficulties as adults, and not all people who have mental health challenges were abused as children. It is not healthy nor is it correct to believe that every case of child abuse leads to permanent damage and long-term suffering. There is, however, a tendency in those who have experience abuse as children to have some of the behaviors and conditions listed below. In the case of abuse, these tendencies can be overcome and dealt with effectively using a variety of the methods in this book, professional counseling and therapy, and guidance from trusted spiritual leaders.

Emotional and Mental Effects of Abuse

Abused children learn that their world is an unpredictable place. A child may develop the attitude that he or she is incompetent, bad, and unworthy. They may learn to distrust close relationships and be wary or suspicious of others. Abused children may learn to deny emotional responses or even disassociate at times from the world.

Adults who have been sexually abused as children may feel anxious feelings of powerlessness, betrayal, and being out of control. If the abuse was within the child's family, a sense of betrayal from the abusive parent or sibling or betrayal on the part of non-abusive parents for failing to provide protection may develop.

Adult child-abuse survivors report more symptoms of fear, anxiety, isolation, depression, and a perception of lower self-worth than others. As children or as adults, victims of abuse report more sleep disturbances, nightmares, and phobias than the average person. Years after the abuse, some abuse victims exhibit symptoms such as dissociation, nervousness, and flashbacks commonly associated with post-traumatic stress disorder.

Abused children may report psychosomatic complaints, including headaches, stomach aches, bed wetting, excessive blinking, general fearfulness, social withdrawal, dissociation, intrusive thoughts, anger, hostility, and guilt. Other behaviors linked to abuse as a child may included things such as difficulty in resolving social problems, self-destructive behaviors, running away behavior, delinquency, early use of drugs/alcohol, eating disorders, and a loss of faith in themselves, others, and God.

There is evidence that children with early traumatic abuse have an increase of dendritic growth in the brain, creating higher sensitivity and increased stress reactions. This change in brain development can create permanent consequences on how an individual responds to challenges or dangers. Their hypersensitivity can make them susceptible to anxiety. While this may be a challenge to learn to manage, it can also be a benefit. Take for instance the African antelope.

Wildlife experts believe about ten percent of the antelopes in a herd are more sensitive to stimuli and danger than the other 90 percent. It is one of the antelopes in this ten percent that always sets off a stampede when danger is present. Without the oversensitive group, the other antelopes in the herd wouldn't survive.

If traumatic experiences as a child have increased your susceptibility to stress and anxiety, this sensitivity may turn into one of your strengths. Once you have learned to manage your increased sensitivity and reduce anxiety, you will find you have an innate understanding and awareness that others do not have. You may find that you recognize signals from others that most people fail to see.

All of the techniques outlined in this book are useful and effective in managing anxiety related to childhood trauma, such as abuse. For example, connecting with your child-like self can be very effective in help speed healing from abuse.

The next few sections contain a few key points about healing from the effects of abuse as a child. While these sections are brief, it does not mean healing from abuse will be quick and easy. For some it may take time and patience. One thing I firmly believe is that the healing will come. I have seen it over and over in my practice as a psychologist.

Disclose the Abuse Appropriately

When evil of any sort is perpetrated upon a child, it is felt physically, emotionally, and spiritually. A child's spirit shuns abuse as evil and the child feels a strange, repulsive feeling inside. Because children can't discern between feeling "yucky" and being "bad" themselves, they often misinterpret abuse and being something that makes them a "bad" child rather than understanding something terrible happened to them.

Children need to be reassured that they are not "bad" because of the abuse that was perpetrated upon them, even if they participated willingly. Most children cannot discern that sexual touch is wrong, especially when someone they trust is telling them it is acceptable. A child may feel he or she deserves to be hit. A child who suffers from neglect believes that if he or she were better, a neglectful parent would love him or her more.

Many times abuse is kept secret for years and years. This secrecy only compounds the shame and guilt typically felt by its victims. Communicating painful memories or tragic life experiences is difficult. The analogy of the splinter helps children understand why it is so important to get out a "painful" secret.

We have all had the uncomfortable experience of having a splinter in our hand. To allow the splinter to stay in place creates soreness, infection, and discomfort. To eliminate the splinter requires that it be pulled out, which can be painful. Removing the splinter creates acute pain, yet letting it remain creates chronic pain.

If we leave the splinter in, we may not use the hand. It may get infected and be even more painful. Every time we touch the area with the splinter it hurts, so we avoid it. It can limit our productivity and overall comfort. When the sharp pain of disclosure is over, the area that housed the splinter can finally heal and life will go on more joyful than before.

Avoid Blame or Revenge

Avoid blaming others for your stress or anxiety linked to childhood abuse. There is a tendency to start blaming others (not the perpetrator) for the effects of the abuse experienced as a child.

Blaming others gives away our power to act and move toward controlling the situation or changing it for the better. We only have so much time and energy in this life. Using our time to cast stones, no matter how well deserved, is a waste of energy and stops our personal growth. Forgiveness is one of the greatest gifts we can give to ourselves. It frees our mind and heart and allows us to move forward.

There is a story told of a man walking through a grassy field in early summer. Without warning he was bitten by a poisonous snake. He was faced with the chance to chase down and kill the snake or stop and suck the poison from his own body. Chasing the snake would push the poison throughout his own body, endangering his life. He chose to pull the poison from his wound and heal himself.

We have choices regarding where we want to put our energy and efforts that greatly affect our emotional well being. Healing is more important than revenge. Channeling our efforts to grow personally is something we can control. We cannot control the actions of others, nor do we want to give them any more power in our lives.

Through avoiding blame and revenge and eventual finding forgiveness, victims of abuse can learn for themselves that they are worthwhile loved individuals. Healing from abuse may take place a piece at a time. The following was written by a woman who was sexually abused for years by a mentally ill father:

> *As an adult, memories of the abuse I experienced as a child terrified me and made me sick. One night, when my husband was out of town, I was lying in bed when I started to feel an unusual floating feeling. I sometimes feel this way before a memory of my childhood abuse surfaces. I remember thinking, 'Oh no, not tonight. I just want to go to sleep.' But the memory came anyway.*
>
> *I felt I was in a pit engulfed by pain with no way to climb out. The pain was so excruciating to my soul that I felt I could not endure another second. My only thought was to pray. I could no longer deal with the horrible pain.*

Then, all of sudden, instead of being at the scene of the abuse, I was somewhere playing. I knew I was home. I was happy and carefree, and I remember feeling so safe. I was only concerned with playing.

There were two women standing behind me. I knew that I was their sole responsibility, and they watched over me constantly. Behind them I could see endless people who seemed happy and at peace. I had a child's mind and was not concerned with what was going on around me. I seemed to be very familiar with everything around me, including the game I was playing.

Then the two women told me it was time to go back. I looked at them very matter-of-factly and said, "I don't want to go back. No one loves me there." The two women looked at each other worriedly. They then took me to a garden, and Jesus was sitting on a bench.

I could feel His love for me, and how glad He was to see me. I had His complete attention. I was telling Him something and He started laughing so joyfully. Then He embraced me and I knew He missed me so much. I felt safe, warm, and happy; happier than I had ever felt in my life!

All of a sudden I was back in my home as a child. I could see myself being abused. However, I was not in my body. Jesus was with me holding my hand. We stood together, waiting for the abuse to stop. Jesus was not going to send me back to my body until it was over. I felt this very clearly. I could feel a conflict within Him. He didn't want me to go back but knew I needed to because I had so much more life in me.

Then I found myself back in the present. My emotional pain was gone. This experience has helped in so many ways. I had always felt lost and unloved by my family, so I had thought Jesus didn't love me either. However, I now know that I am loved, and that I have a purpose in life.

Finding a purpose in life often leads to the ultimate healing from abuse. To move forward is a glorious thing. It is not easy, and to completely recover takes much effort. But there is help. There are many books and programs to get you started. Mental health professionals are typically well-trained in helping others get through the grief and shame of abuse. Answers are available. Trust that as you seek them, a loving Father in Heaven will give you the strength needed to attain peace.

ABOUT THE AUTHORS:

Dr. Victoria Anderson is a licensed psychologist who currently practices in California and Utah. She received her doctorate in psychology in 1989. She has lectured throughout the Western United States on varied subjects in the mental health field. She is a contributing author for the book *Confronting Abuse*. Dr. Anderson has seen hundreds of people change their lives using the principles found in this book.

Lois D. Brown received her bachelor's in journalism and a master's degree in communications. She has worked in Washington, D.C., as a news correspondent and in Utah as a corporate communications specialist. Since becoming a freelance writer, she has written both non-fiction and fiction books. Visit her at: www.loisdbrown.com.

ENDNOTES

---

[1] Gordon B. Hinckley. *Way to Be*, Simon & Schuster, 2002.
[2] Simpkinson, Anne A. "Is There a Therapist in the House?" Prevention. http://www.prevention.com
[3] Marra, Thomas. *Depressed and Anxious*, New Harbinger Publications: Oakland, California, 2004.
[4] Hawkins, R.S., S.-Y. Tan, and A.A. Turk, "Secular Versus Christian Inpatient Cognitive-Behavioral Therapy Programs : Impact on Depression and Spiritual Well-Being," *Journal of Psychology and Theology*, 1999. 27 (Wint 1999): p. 309-31.
[5] *Ensign*, November 2002. p. 37.
[6] Douglas Hunt, MD, "No More Fears," Warner Books, New York, NY, 1988.
[7] David V. Sheehan, MD, "The Anxiety Disease," Bantam Books, New York, NY, 1986.
[8] Bourne, Edward, Ph.D. and Lorna Garano. *Coping with Anxiety: Ten simple ways to relieve anxiety, fear and worry*. New Harbinger Publications: Oakland, California, 2003.
[9] Bourne, Edmund J., Ph.D. *The Anxiety & Phobia Workbook 3rd Edition*, New Harbinger Publications, Inc. 2000.
[10] Raeburn, Paul. "A Case for Double-Edged Optimism: The new rules of the immunity game," PsychologyToday.com, http://www.psychologytoday.com/articles/pto-20060424-000002.html
[11] Scott, James Coleman. "Psychology and Effective Behavior," Foresman and Company: Glenview, Illinois, 1969, p. 269.
[12] Morrison, Alexander B. "Some Myths and Misconceptions About Mental Illness," Presented *to Pioneer Welfare Region Leaders*, in Salt Lake City UT, April 21, 2001.
[13] DSM IV
[14] Osmond, Marie and Marcia Wilkie, Dr. Judith Moore. *Behind the Smile: My Journey out of Postpartum Depression*. Warner Books: New York, 2001.

[15] Skarnulils, Leanna. "Silent Risk: Women and Heart Disease," *Health* .msn.com, Jan. 26, 2004.
[16] *Journal of Neuroscience*, January 21, 2004.
[17] "Questions and Answers," *Tambuli*, Oct. 1988, p. 10.
[18] Morrison, Alexander B. "Some Myths and Misconceptions About Mental Illness," Presented *to Pioneer Welfare Region Leaders*, in Salt Lake City UT, April 21, 2001.
[19] Jorm, Anthony F. et al. "Effectiveness of complementary and self-help treatments for anxiety disorders," *Medical Journal of Australia*, 2004; 181 (7): S29-S46.
[20] Lippincotts Prim Care Pract. 1999 May-Jun;3(3):290-304.
[21] Ibid.
[22] Widtsoe, John A. ed. *Discourses of Brigham Young*. Deseret Book: Salt Lake City, 1954, 163.
[23] *Ensign*, October 2003.
[24] Bourne, Edward, Ph.D. and Lorna Garano. *Coping with Anxiety: Ten simple ways to relieve anxiety, fear and worry*. New Harbinger Publications: Oakland, California, 2003.
[25] Carmack, Cindy et al. *Ann Behav Med* 21:251-257, 1999.
[26] www.bidmc.haravard.edu.
[27] The Lancet, December 7, 2002; 360:1840-1842.
[28] Field, Ironson, Pickens et al. "Massage therapy reduces anxiety and enhances EEG pattern of alertness and math computations," *International Journal of Neuroscience,* 1996, pp. 86, 197-205.
[29] Chisholm, K. A three year follow-up of attachment and indiscriminate friendliness in children adopted from Romanian orphanages. Child Development, 69, 1998, 1092 – 1106.
[30] Hart, Sybil et al. Eating Disorders: The Journal of Treatment and Prevention, 2001, Vol. 9, pp. 217-228.
[31] Wolff, Lothar. *Rock A Bye Baby*. A *Time Life* Documentary, 1970.
[32] McGrath, Ellen. "Learning to Recover: When life hands you a setback, readjust your identity," PsychologyToday.com, http://www.psychologytoday.com/articles/pto-20030619-000001.html
[33] McPherson, Tammy. The Daily Herald, November 7, 2003.
[34] Gordon B. Hinckley. *Way to Be*, Simon & Schuster, 2002.

[35] Covey, Stephen. *Seven Habits of Successful People*, Simon & Schuster, 1989.
[36] L. Brent Goates, *Harold B. Lee: Prophet and Seer,* Bookcraft: Salt Lake City, Utah, 1985.
[37] Fielding, Lavina. "The Long Odyssey," *Ensign*, Feb. 1974, p. 8.
[38] See Bible Dictionary "Jonah"
[39] Bolmon, Lee G. and Terrence E. Deal. *Leading with Soul*, Jassey-bass Publishers, San Francisco, 1995, p. 32.
[40] Wilson, Reid R. *Don't Panic: Taking Control of Anxiety Attacks*, HarperCollins Publisher: New York, 1996, p. 243.
[41] Kikuchi, Yoshihiko. "Do We Know How Much He Went Through?" Devotional lecture delivered at *LDS Business College*, Oct. 14, 1998.
[42] Kalb, Claudia. "Faith and Healing," *Newsweek*, Nov 10, 2003.
[43] James E. Faust, "Strengthening the Inner Self," *Liahona,* Feb. 2003, p. 3.
[44] Ibid.
[45] Hawkins, R.S., S.-Y. Tan, and A.A. Turk, "Secular Versus Christian Inpatient Cognitive-Behavioral Therapy Programs : Impact on Depression and Spiritual Well-Being," *Journal of Psychology and Theology*, Winter 1999, 27: p. 309-31.
[46] Morrison, Alexander B. "Some Myths and Misconceptions About Mental Illness," Presented *to Pioneer Welfare Region Leaders*, in Salt Lake City UT, April 21, 2001.
[47] Kalb, Claudia. "Faith and Healing," *Newsweek*, Nov 10, 2003.
[48] Borysenko, Joan Ph.D. *Minding the Body, Mending the Mind*, pp. 11-112.
[49] *Teachings of the Presidents of the Church: Heber J. Grant*, The Church of Jesus Christ of Latter-day Saints: SLC, Utah, 2002.
[50] Benson, Herbert. *The Relaxation Response*, HarperTorch, 1976.
[51] *McCall's Magazine,* December, 1998.
[52] Benson, Ezra T, "Do Not Despair," *Tambuli*, Mar. 1987, p. 2.
[53] "Behold, We Count Them Happy Which Endure," *Ensign*, May 1998, p. 77.
[54] http://en.wikiquote.org/wiki/Mahatma_Gandhi
[55] Ibid.
[56] *Ensign,* Feb. 1995, p. 32.

---

[57] Ashton, Marvin J. "Roadblocks to Progress," *Ensign,* May 1979, p. 67.
[58] Kimball, Spencer W. *The Miracle of Forgivenes,* Deseret Book: SLC, 1969, p. 363.
[59] Kin, N.W. & V.M. Sanders. "It Takes Nerve to Tell T and B Cells What to Do," *Journal of Leukocyte Biology*, June: 79(6), 2006, pp. 1093-1104.
[60] Hashizuma, H. & M. Takigawa. "Anxiety in Allergy and Atopic Dermatitis," *Current Opinion in Allergy and Clinical Immunology*, Oct: 6(5), 2006, pp. 335-336.
[61] McConkie, Bruce R. *Devotional Speeches of the Year,* Provo, Utah: Brigham Young University, 1979, pp. 399-400.
[62] Hughes, Kathleen H. "Blessed by Living Water," *Ensign,* May 2003, p. 13.
[63] Hawkins, R.S., S.-Y. Tan, and A.A. Turk, *"Secular Versus Christian Inpatient Cognitive-Behavioral Therapy Programs : Impact on Depression and Spiritual Well-Being," Journal of Psychology and Theology,* Winter 1999, 27: p. 309-31.
[64] Rapee, Ronald M., Susan H. Spence, Vanessa Cobham, and Ann Wignall. *Helping Your Anxious Child: A Step-by-stop Guide for Parents*, New Harbinger Publications: Oakland, California, 2000.
[65] Field, T., Hernandez-Reif, M., Hart, S., Quintino, O., Drose, L., Field, T., Kuhn, C. & Schanberg, S. Effects of sexual abuse are lessened by massage therapy. *Journal of Bodywork and Movement Therapies*, 1997, 1: p. 65 – 69.
[66] U.S. Department of Health and Human Services, Administration for Children and Families, Administration on Children, Youth and Families, Children's Bureau. (2011). Child Maltreatment 2010.
[67] *The Health of Adolescent Boys: Commonwealth Fund Survey Findings.* New York, NY: The Commonwealth Fund, 1998.
[68] *The Commonwealth Fund Survey of the Health of Adolescent Girls.* New York, NY: The Commonwealth Fund, 1997.
[69] Murdock, Maxine. "Hope and Healing," *Ensign*, Jan. 1993, p. 62.
[70] Hinckley, Gordon B. "Save the Children," *Ensign,* Nov. 1994, p. 52.

66075827R00124

Made in the USA
San Bernardino, CA
08 January 2018